MEN
LEADING
THE CHARGE

GOD'S GAME PLAN
FOR THE FAMILY

STEVE FARRAR

LifeWay Press
Nashville, Tennessee

This book along with the video is the text for course CG-0605
in the study area Personal Life in the Christian Growth Study Plan.

Unless otherwise noted, Scripture quotations are from the Holy Bible, *New International Version*,
copyright © 1973, 1978, 1984 by International Bible Society.
Scripture quotations marked (NLT) are taken from the *Holy Bible,* New Living Translation, copyright © 1996.
Used by permission of Tyndale House Publishers, Inc., Wheaton, Illinois 60189. All rights reserved.

Some references are attributed to the following books by Steve Farrar:
Point Man (Sisters, OR: Multnomah Books, 1990)
Standing Tall (Sisters, OR: Multnomah Books, 1994)
Finishing Strong (Sisters, OR: Multnomah Books, 1995)
Anchor Man (Nashville, TN: Thomas Nelson, 1998)

To order additional copies of this resource:
WRITE LifeWay Church Resources Customer Service; 127 Ninth Avenue, North; Nashville, TN 37234-0113;
FAX order to (615) 251-5933; PHONE 1-800-458-2772; EMAIL to *CustomerService@lifeway.com*
ONLINE at *www.lifeway.com;*or visit the LifeWay Christian Store serving you.

For information about adult discipleship and family resources, training, and events,
visit our Web site at *www.lifeway.com/discipleplus.*

Published in association with the literary agency of Alive Communications, Inc.;
1465 Kelly Johnson Blvd., #320; Colorado Springs, CO 80920.

Design: Bob Redden
Curriculum Writer: Larry Keefauver

Printed in the United States of America

LifeWay Press
127 Ninth Avenue, North
Nashville, Tennessee 37234-0151

*As God works through us, we will help people and churches know Jesus Christ
and seek His kingdom by providing biblical solutions that spiritually transform individuals and cultures.*

Contents

About the Author

Dr. Steve Farrar is the founder and chairman of Men's Leadership Ministries. Steve speaks to thousands of men each year at his Men's Spiritual Leadership Conferences, which are specifically designed to equip men to become more effective spiritual leaders for their families. He believes men want to be successful, significant, and find meaning in their lives. "Men want to be good husbands, good fathers, and the spiritual leaders of their families," he says, "but the problem is, many of them don't know how to do these things." This desperate need gave Dr. Farrar the passion and vision for equipping men for spiritual leadership.

A graduate of California State University, Fullerton, Farrar majored in Speech Communication. He holds a Master's degree from Western Seminary in Portland, Oregon, and a doctorate from Dallas Theological Seminary in Dallas, Texas. In writing his doctoral dissertation, Farrar surveyed over one thousand men from across the nation, and questioned them about their marriages, children, careers, and ethics. His research into Christian men's needs became the basis for his conferences and books.

Dr. Farrar is the author of the best-selling book, *Point Man: How a Man Can Lead His Family.* With over 300,000 copies in print and now translated into Spanish and Korean, *Point Man* was the catalyst for Dr. Farrar's leaving the pastorate after 15 years and focusing his ministry on equipping men for spiritual leadership. Shortly after the release of *Point Man,* Dr. Farrar began to receive speaking invitations from all over the nation. "Quite frankly, the response was overwhelming," says Dr. Farrar. "We received over 350 speaking requests during the first year of the book's release." Dr. Farrar never intended to speak exclusively to men, but it quickly became apparent that a pressing need existed for his message in *Point Man,* and now his subsequent books to men about spiritual leadership in all aspects of their lives.

Since the release of *Point Man* in 1990, Dr. Farrar has also authored *Standing Tall: How a Man Can Protect His Family* (1994), *Finishing Strong: Finding the Power to Go the Distance* (1995), *Anchor Man: How a Father Can Anchor His Family in Christ for the Next 100 Years* (1998), *Quiet Whispers from God's Heart* (1999), and his latest book, *Get in the Ark: Finding Safety in the Coming Judgment.* Dr. Farrar is also a frequent speaker for Men's Leadership Ministries' conferences, Promise Keepers, and many other events throughout the nation.

Steve's wife, Mary, attended Western Seminary and published the best-selling book, *Choices: For Women Who Long to Discover Life's Best.* The Farrars have three children and currently reside in Dallas, Texas. Held nationwide, Steve's conferences are designed to "equip men in personal character and holiness who are thus qualified to lead the family, the church, and the nation in our time of acute moral and spiritual crisis." Dr. Farrar's unique teaching is often humorous, always biblical and challenging, highly insightful, and full of practical advice designed to give men the tools they need to become all that God intends them to be.

Introduction

We live in a confusing, high-pressure, and difficult culture for men. Christian men who seriously seek to provide spiritual leadership in their families often don't know how. In the accompanying video lectures, Steve Farrar talks to men about both the need for and the practical aspects of men leading their families.

This study book provides a daily follow-up for five days of study after each video session. In the workbook you will explore more deeply into the subjects Steve talks about. The topics will include: the need for husbands and fathers to provide leadership in the home, how to be a godly husband to your wife, how to anchor your family in Christ for the next hundred years, and how to be a godly father.

In the final half of the study Steve deals with some specialized issues facing modern fathers. He discusses childrearing in this gender-confused age. Steve provides help for confronting the relativism that has devastated both modern society and families. He dedicates a session to one of the greatest struggles facing men: how to be a one-woman kind of man. Finally Steve focuses on the ultimate goal for every Christian man—finishing your journey strong for Christ.

Each week we encourage you to meet with your men's group to view and discuss Steve's video sessions. Then study each day the material in this workbook. Make the study part of your daily quiet time. Make notes of issues you want to study further in your personal Bible study.

For each video session you will find a viewer guide in this book. Use the viewer guide to help you to take notes as you watch the video presentations. In the back of the book you will find group discussion questions to go along with each session of the video series. If you are leading the study, you will want to use the group discussion questions to follow each video. Even if you are not leading the group, familiarize yourself with the questions so you will better be able to participate in discussion of the video.

The days in which we live cry out for Christian men to provide godly leadership. Our society is filled with false images of what it means to be a man. We see abusive and neglectful husbands and fathers. We see weak and ineffective men. We see men who ignore their wives and children while they concentrate on job and career. Dr. Steve Farrar wants to challenge you to provide a different kind of model for the families of our day. He wants to challenge you to be a Christian man who leads your family with both courage and tenderness. Now is the time for men to lead the charge.

WEEK 1

POINT MAN ON PATROL– THE NECESSITY OF GODLY MALE LEADERSHIP

VIEWER GUIDE

The endangered species about which I am concerned is the _____ _____ in the home—

the man who knows what it means to lead his family spiritually before Jesus Christ.

Leadership is central to the well-being of a ...

- _____

- _____

- _____

We have a leadership crisis in America. Leadership is ultimately an issue of the _____.

_____ comes from a person's heart.

_____ comes from a person's heart.

Ultimately, _____ is always an issue of the heart.

Fathers are the _____ _____ (reference point) of their families.

_____ is our reference point.

As we follow Christ, we're giving our kids a compass—_____—that will get them through

the chaos and confusion that surrounds them on a daily basis.

"A _____ is someone who _____."

1. Satan wants to _____ and eventually _____ the relationship you have with your wife.

2. Satan wants to _____ and eventually _____ the relationship you have with your kids.

DAY 1
Godly Men: An Endangered Species

Read Ephesians 5:23-25.

Almost everyone has heard of endangered species. On the list are animals such as the blue whale, the bald eagle, condors, and the snail darter. What you will not find on that list is one creature that is rapidly disappearing from our modern world: the godly man—the spiritual leader in the home. Sure, you can go just about anywhere and find "guys," but how often do you find a man who not only knows God's principles but also practices them?

In Christian homes across America today, many men will read Ephesians 5 and feel they are doing fine. Their wives seem content, and their children appear happy and well adjusted.
- Are these men truly leading their families as Christ leads the church?
- Are they the "point man" in their homes?
- Do they lead their families by example as well as by words?

The Christian family is in a war, and the man is the prime target of the enemy. The man is the primary target because he is the natural leader of the family.

So how are American men doing? Some interesting facts in *Point Man* shed some light on our record:
- One out of two marriages ends in divorce.
- In 1996, two out of every five households were maintained by women, with no husband present.
- Tonight enough teenagers to fill the Rose Bowl, Cotton Bowl, Sugar Bowl, Orange Bowl, Fiesta Bowl, and the average Super Bowl will practice prostitution to support drug addictions.
- One million teenage girls will get pregnant out of wedlock this year.
- Five hundred thousand of those girls will abort their babies.
- Sixty percent of all church-involved teenagers are sexually active.
- Sixty-six percent of American high-school seniors have used illegal drugs.
- Every 78 seconds, a teenager in America attempts suicide (*Point Man*, 17-18).

These facts are alarming. Maintaining a godly family in today's society can be daunting. Many men fail; they intend to do well, but come up short.

What situations have affected your efforts to have a godly family? I have: (check all that may apply)
- ❏ been divorced.
- ❏ engaged in immoral activities.
- ❏ given in to cultural morals.
- ❏ maintained an excessive work schedule.
- ❏ had poor role models.
- ❏ (other) _____

The Good News

Thankfully, we have good news. We have a God who is good to us; He has given us His Word to follow and Himself as an example. Ephesians 5:23 says, "The husband is the head of the wife as Christ is the head of the church, his body, of which he is the Savior."

As men, it is our privilege and our responsibility to be the head of the family. God has not asked women to assume this role, and He will not hold them accountable for the task men have been given. As a man, you have to be active and intentional about your family. You do not have the luxury of being lazy. The devil is looking for idle hands. You must actively model Christ to your family so they too will follow Christ.

So how do you lead your family to follow Christ? Ephesians 5:25 says, "Husbands, love your wives, just as Christ loved the church and gave himself up for her." Sacrificial love is the answer. A love that is "as strong as death" (Song of Songs 8:6). Permit me to ask you some hard questions about your relationship to your family.
- What evidence shows that you love your wife?
- You may take care of your children's physical needs, but what about their spiritual and emotional needs?
- You love your wife enough to die for her, but will you control your thoughts and your eyes for her?
- You love your children, but will you show them what it means to be a godly husband and father?

In the following list, circle each area in which you feel you are doing well:

providing financially	prayer	sexual purity
reading Scripture	time with family	encouragement
intimacy	conversation	household chores

Chances are, you have discovered at least one or two areas that could use some improvement. The task now is to begin, with Christ's help, to be all you can be as a husband and father.

Choose one of the areas above in which you feel some inadequacy. Underline it.

What is one specific action you can take to improve in that area today? _____

_____

If God has given you a wife and children, He wants you to enjoy them and help them enter fully into His kingdom. Make today a new beginning on the road to becoming a Christlike family. God has promised to be with you, and will help you.

Write a one-sentence prayer. Ask God for strength and help in being a "leading" man.

_____

_____

DAY 2
Definition of a Leader

Read Mark 10:42-45.

What is a leader? By definition, a leader is someone who leads. It's interesting that this definition does not say someone who gives commands or someone who has power. A leader is someone who leads.

Write down the names of four men you consider to be true leaders:

_____   _____

_____   _____

Now, think about the characteristics of each of these men.
- What do they have in common?
- Have they been successful leaders in the eyes of the world?
- Are they leading by example or merely by what they say?
- Are they leading as God intends?

Mark 10:43 (NLT) says, "Whoever wants to be a leader among you must be your servant." Recall the list above. As you thought of leaders, did you think about the characteristic of servanthood? God speaks the truth to us when He says that a true leader must first be a servant. Christ is the supreme example of true leadership. If you want to know how to lead, follow Christ.

Scripture compares a man's relationship with his wife to Christ's relationship to the church. Christ's example of leadership began with self-sacrifice.
- Christ set aside His glory and took on the form of a servant.
- Christ gave us His Word.
- Christ sacrificed His own life that we might live.

You can apply each of the examples above to your family. You can humble yourself and serve your wife and children. You can give your family God's truth through what you say and do. You can sacrifice your own desires and pleasures for your family's good.

How do you sacrifice for your family? At the top of the next page you will find a series of family issues. For each category place an X on the line indicating the amount of sacrifice you now make:

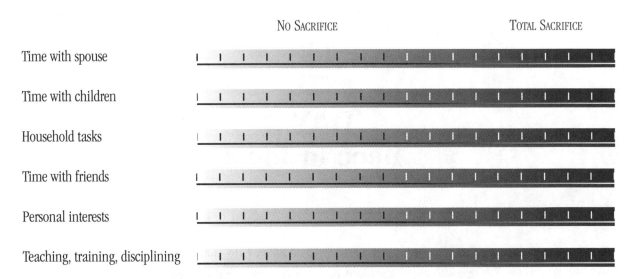

The goal of any family leader is to meet his responsibilities. Obviously, you must provide financially for your family, but God has appointed you to provide in many other ways as well.

- You provide emotional support as well as companionship to your wife.
- You provide discipline and love for your children.
- You are a spiritual role model for your entire family.

All too often, men think that if they put food on the table, they have done their duty. We need to continually remember that our families have emotional and spiritual needs that no amount of money or security can fulfill. Just as God provides for all of our needs, you should, with God's help, provide more than money for your family.

Satan wants to neutralize you as your family's leader. Just as a team is made ineffective by losing a star player, your family is made ineffective if you are a passive leader. A leader is one who leads. Don't let your family be the enemy's victims.

Before you can be a great leader, you must first be a great follower. Determine that you will follow Christ. Christ said, " 'Therefore everyone who hears these words of mine and puts them into practice is like a wise man who built his house on the rock,' " (Matt. 7:24). When we follow Christ, we're building spiritual homes. Raising our kids on the secure Rock of Jesus Christ demonstrates that we're leaders and, more importantly, that we're followers of Christ and our future is secure.

Complete the following prayer, asking for God's help in making you the leader He wants you to be.

Father, help me lead my family as Christ would by _____

_____

_____.

Begin now to learn how to sacrifice for your family. List one practical way you can practice sacrificial love this week:

_____

DAY 3
Keep in Touch

Read Hebrews 13:1-5.

"Never will I fail you; never will I forsake you" (Heb. 13:5), God said to us through Scripture. He is the ultimate Father figure. While He is the only One who will never fail, men should strive to be faithful. Being a husband and father is a calling requiring great determination and perseverance.

Have you made a commitment to stay with your family no matter what? Give one example from last month of your commitment to your family.

_____

A Chinese proverb says, "It is harder to lead a family than to rule a nation." What makes this vocation so difficult?

_____

Satan has a two-fold strategy for destroying your family:
　　Strategy 1: *To effectively alienate and sever a husband's relationship with his wife.*
　　Strategy 2: *To effectively alienate and sever a father's relationship with his children (Point Man, 21).*

The enemy can't destroy a family without first separating husband and wife. If he successfully alienates the two of you either physically or emotionally, he knows your family is on the brink of destruction. The difficult part is recognizing how alienation begins and eventually grows into separation. Ask yourself these questions:

EMOTIONAL
- How often do I think of my wife's emotional needs?
- How often do I ask my wife what she's thinking?
- How often do I compliment my wife for doing something well?
- When I am feeling down, to whom do I go for encouragement?

- When I have a problem, do I ask my wife's opinion?
- How often do we pray together?
- When did I last surprise my wife with a gift?
- Do I listen to my wife with compassion and care?

PHYSICAL
- When I am not at work, how do I spend most of my time?
- Do we try to find mutually entertaining activities?
- Do I look my wife in the eye when we talk?

- When did I last take my wife on a date?
- Do we eat meals together?
- How often do I hold my wife's hand or give her an affectionate hug?

Separation occurs at many levels, and the enemy is trying to drive a wedge between you and your wife. Perhaps you have become emotionally separated without even realizing it. It doesn't take much to become neutralized in your relationship, and it doesn't always end with your spouse. If the enemy successfully separates you from your wife, it is only a matter of time before he targets your children. Proverbs 20:7 says, "The righteous man leads a blameless life; blessed are his children after him." God chooses to work through you to raise righteous children. If you are absent emotionally or physically, your children will suffer the consequences.

A godly man will persevere and stay unified with his wife and children. *Point Man* cites a survey of more than one thousand kids attending Joe White's Christian camp. Most came from homes where the father and mother were in a committed, loving relationship:

- Ninety-five percent of the boys say their fathers regularly tell them, "I love you."
- Ninety-eight percent of the girls say their mothers tell them regularly, "I'm proud of you" or "You're doing a great job."
- Ninety-one percent say their parents play games with them regularly.
- Ninety-seven percent say they get hugs from their dads.
- One hundred percent of the girls say their parents have taken them to Sunday School (*Point Man,* 25).

More than 80 percent of these kids are opposed to sex before marriage, and 92 percent say they do not use illegal drugs. The families of the majority of these kids keep in touch. Their fathers are present when they need love or discipline.

How well do you relate to your children? How much time do you spend with your children in a week? ____ hours
Do you know your children's likes and dislikes? If so, list a few of them.

	LIKES	DISLIKES
Child 1:	_____	_____
Child 2:	_____	_____
Child 3:	_____	_____

Do you know your kids' ambitions? (circle one)   Yes   No

The enemy will use good things such as ministry and our work to distract us from our primary task. Do not become passive; we must not allow the enemy to neutralize us. The best, most effective family leader is a follower of Jesus Christ. (See 1 Tim. 3.) The closer we draw to Christ, the more effective we will become.

A father's most important task is to keep in touch with his family. Write a short prayer, asking for God's help in staying in touch with your family. Then do the hard part—keep in touch.

_____

_____

_____

DAY 4
Neutral Gets You Nowhere

Read 1 Timothy 4:6-13.

How often have you heard a pastor compare the Christian life to a spa? Have you heard him describe it as a soothing, relaxing place where you are pampered and coddled, where your every need is instantaneously met? Chances are, you won't hear such a comparison. The Christian life is anything but soothing and relaxing. Look at Jesus' life.

The man who is living a Christian life is on a journey that begins the moment he is born again and will not end until he enters the life to come. He can be certain the enemy will stop at nothing to keep him from arriving at his destination. Satan wants him to relax and take it easy. In other words, Satan wants him to put it in neutral.

Often, the enemy doesn't have to do anything. We are either too lazy to keep going or we are simply asleep, unaware of our own spiritual condition. Christ calls these Christians *lukewarm*. They are neither hot nor cold. Satan would prefer everyone to be lukewarm, because neutral Christians represent no challenge to him.

Satan wants to neutralize those men who are working hard at being biblical husbands and fathers. The enemy hates men who love their wives and who raise godly children. He knows that they threaten his power and control.

How is your spiritual condition? One of the best ways to evaluate your spirituality is to determine your priorities. Prioritizing your time to become and remain spiritually fit really matters.

Answer the following questions with the amount of time you spend on each activity:

I spend _____ minutes per day reading and meditating on Scripture.

I spend _____ minutes per day in prayer.

I spend _____ minutes per day in devotions with my family.

You may be thinking time is not really that important, but time is one of our most valuable commodities. How you spend your time directly reveals the attitude of your heart. Simply thinking you are doing fine means nothing. Actually sacrificing your time to condition your spiritual body is the only way to spiritual health.

We are told to exercise aerobically at least 30 minutes three times per week to insure a strong heart. Can a heart for the Lord be built in less time?

The importance of spiritual health cannot be overstated. You obviously need to think of your own well-being, but you need to think of your family even more. Remember that Satan wants to neutralize you. He knows that if you are out of the way, your family is a much easier target. Just as an army without a leader is confused and ineffective, your family without your spiritual leadership is open to the attacks of the enemy.

Your physical body needs certain things to be healthy. It needs the right nutrition and plenty of exercise, and you should avoid dangerous habits. Your spiritual body is no different. It needs to have a healthy diet of God's Word. It needs to be strengthened through spiritual exercise.

The best way to grow spiritually is by disciplining yourself to establish spiritual good habits. Read Scripture and pray every day. You may need to change your lifestyle in order to find time for your relationship with God.

In the following spaces, write your plan for setting a definite time and place to do each of these activities:

	WHEN	WHERE
Bible reading	_____	_____
time in prayer	_____	_____
family devotions	_____	_____

Spiritual conditioning begins with the Bible and prayer, but it doesn't end there. It must be put into practice. Just as athletes work to get off the bench and into the game, you have to practice the Christian life.

Perhaps you are doing well with your spiritual condition, but need to focus on perseverance. You will experience many peaks and valleys in your life. The goal is always to keep on toward the finish line. The enemy waits for you to let your guard down. Don't give him the satisfaction.

Write a brief prayer, asking for wisdom in adjusting your lifestyle to accommodate more time for building a meaningful relationship with God through prayer and Bible study. Pray that God will help you grow in love for Him and His Word.

_____

_____

_____

_____

DAY 5
The Reality of Sin

Read 1 Corinthians 10:1-13.

This world is often unpleasant. Watch the evening news and count how many times murder, rape, war, or violence is mentioned in a single broadcast. The hearts of men are hardened toward God, and the whole world suffers.

As a Christian man, you have been given a great gift—the gift of salvation. God loves you passionately and wants you to be with Him for all eternity. So why do we allow the cares of this world to turn our attention away from Him and away from becoming what we are capable of being?

Think about the verses you read from 1 Corinthians. Why a people who saw God's mighty hand so plainly chose to turn to their own way is hard to understand, but the fact is, we are no different. We see God's love for us plainly and yet we also turn to idols, immorality, pride, and complaining. We too are wandering in a desert as we search for the promised land.

Understand Your Limits

We often don't recognize temptation when it comes, and we do even less to avoid it. Every day we are tempted by sin. The sins of lust, greed, and bigotry present themselves to us every day. What temptations do you face?

In the following spaces, write three temptations that you faced yesterday and where they occurred.

TEMPTATION   WHERE IT OCCURRED

_____   _____

_____   _____

_____   _____

The temptation to sin can occur any time and anywhere. The reality of life is that we must struggle to avoid sin. You are the target of the enemy, and he is subtle. He knows your weaknesses. He knows how to tempt you. However, you know the One who is greater than all temptation, and you must live in His strength.

Reread verses 12 and 13—God's promise to us as believers. Where we are weak, He is strong. Where we cannot save ourselves, He is waiting to save us. Our task is to recognize Who can help us and follow Him.

Decide how to deal with temptation before you get into a difficult situation. You must be trained for the battle if you expect to win. Training can take several forms, but the most important preparation is to know God's Word. As the psalmist said, "I have hidden your word in my heart that I might not sin against you" (Ps. 119:11).

If you are serious about taking God's Word to heart, you should also be serious about fighting sin. Look back at your list of temptations and where they occurred. In the following spaces, write specific ways of avoiding those temptations. For example, if you were tempted to display your anger in a hurtful way when a colleague made a mistake, decide beforehand that you want to be forgiving. If you were tempted to lust when you were on the Internet, avoid using the Internet when you are alone or subscribe to a filtered Internet service.

To avoid _____, I will _____

To avoid _____, I will _____

To avoid _____, I will _____

You should understand by now that the Christian life is a constant struggle. You must not be caught off guard. You are the point man for your family. To remain strong in your position, you must be determined. Make a decision to stay away from temptation and with God's help to resist sin.

Finish the following prayer of thanksgiving by remembering times when God delivered you from sin. Ask for His strength as you continue to honor Him in your thoughts and actions.

Father God, I thank You that You delivered me from _____

_____

_____

_____

I ask You to give me Your strength as I continue to resist sin's temptation. Guard my heart by ...

_____

_____

_____

_____.

WEEK 2

THE TASKS
OF HUSBANDS

VIEWER GUIDE

Living with our wives in _____ _____ _____ is one of a husband's primary jobs.

"You husbands likewise, live with your wives in an understanding way, as with a weaker vessel, since she is a woman; and grant her honor as a fellow heir of the grace of life, so that your prayers may not be hindered" (1 Pet. 3:7, NASB).

The goal of a Christian life is not just to grow old in Christ; the goal of a Christian life is to _____ ___ in Christ;

The goal is to press on to maturity, to _____ _____ _____.

When our culture says *equality,* it means _____.

Sameness is not equality. God has granted us _____ as men and women before Him.

When a wife does not feel understood, a huge _____ develops into a _____,

that can develop into an _____ _____.

The answer to that depends: How _____ are you?

DAY 1
Marriage Is a Gift

Read Genesis 2:15-25.

God created humankind in His image. Have you ever considered what that exactly means? Underline one or more of the possibilities below or write your own explanation:

God has a nose and ears.
We are spiritual beings.
We are capable of a relationship with the Creator.
We have an intellect that makes us distinct from the plant and animal kingdoms.

_____

In Genesis 1:27, God's image is described as male and female. Genesis 2:24, male and female are united through marriage. In marriage two individuals can tear down barriers and become one. The married life is a unique opportunity to become what God intended for us to be.

However, because of our selfish pride, we often build up, rather than tear down, those barriers that separate us. We create solid walls between us where there should be open space.

Place an X on the line indicating how you feel right now about the oneness of your marriage:

Despair   Delight

Every marriage has its peaks and valleys. Every marriage has good times as well as bad. Let's face it, you are going to face difficulties in your marriage.

When a couple first gets married, they have little idea what is truly in store for them. A newlywed couple may only hear, "for better, for richer, and in health." I once heard that 60 percent of all college graduates believe they will be millionaires by the time they reach 30. Many people think of marriage the same way. It will last forever simply because we love each other. Without hard work and Christ's leadership, couples are bound to be disappointed.

If you have been married for any length of time, you probably realize that it isn't always the way you thought it would be. If you can, try to recall what you thought your marriage would be like. Briefly describe it below.

_____

_____

Remember, though, when you married, you made commitments such as, for better or for worse; for richer or for poorer; in sickness and in health; and till death do us part.

If a commitment is forever, how is it different from a contract? A contract is _____

_____.

A commitment is something you see through to the end. A commitment is something that can't be broken because of hard times. A contract is usually time-dated and has clauses for breaking it.

Marriage is difficult to maintain. In the first session, we discussed the enemy's twofold strategy for tearing down families. The first strategy is to drive a wedge between the husband and wife, eventually severing that relationship. Unfortunately, this strategy works all too often.

Name an issue Satan has used to begin a wedge between you and your wife:_____

This week addresses two of God's strategies for building up families. The first strategy is to live with your wife in an understanding way. We will cover this strategy in day 2. The second strategy is to honor your wife, and we will discuss that strategy on day 5.

This week we will try to understand how God wants us to treat our wives. More importantly, we will begin to practice techniques for building a stronger Christian marriage. With God's help and guidance, we will become stronger husbands to our wives and more godly leaders in our homes. What every Christian husband needs to realize is that marriage is a gift from God, blessed by His Holy Spirit. If God is present in that marriage, not only can it survive, but it can also thrive.

Write a brief prayer, asking God to help you see both the healthy and unhealthy sides of your marriage. Ask Him to give you the strength to build up your marriage in Christ.

_____

_____

_____

_____

DAY 2
Live in an Understanding Way

Read 1 Peter 3:7.

What key words do you see in this verse? Consider underlining them in your Bible. Do words or phrases like *considerate,* and *treat her with respect* appear in your translation?

In the New American Standard translation of 1 Peter 3:7, the verse reads, "You husbands likewise, live with your wives in an understanding way." Recall from week 1 that Satan is trying to alienate you and eventually separate you from your wife. Remember that the enemy never gives up. Whether you have been married seven months, seven years, or seventy years, you need to be aware of the enemy's strategy and have a defense for it.

In His wisdom, God has given us a counter-offensive to combat the enemy. Notice these facts about 1 Peter 3:7. First, it is addressed to husbands. Peter is speaking directly to married men. Second, you will find a twofold counter-offensive that can be used against the enemy in his attempts to sever the relationship you enjoy with your wife. Today we will deal with the first part of God's strategy: live with your wife in an understanding way.

What does this first task of a husband mean? How would you define living in an *understanding way*?

_____

_____

Living in an understanding way is the first counter-offensive to the enemy. If the husband is willing to practice sacrificial love and be sensitive to the differences and needs of his wife, then he will be living in an understanding way. God expects you to live with your wife in an understanding way because that is how He lives with us.

In the following list, check each characteristic that exemplifies living in an understanding way.
- ❑ being patient
- ❑ ignoring your wife's complaints
- ❑ complimenting your wife
- ❑ making decisions alone
- ❑ being respectful
- ❑ repeatedly inconveniencing your wife
- ❑ embarrassing her in public
- ❑ expecting dinner at a certain time
- ❑ desiring to know your wife's opinion
- ❑ making decisions as partners
- ❑ not making amends after an argument
- ❑ listening
- ❑ sharing some of your wife's interests
- ❑ letting her choose first

Living in an understanding way can characterize every area of your marriage. It begins with your being able to recognize who your wife is. She is not you; she is not an extension of you. She is a unique person with whom you have been joined. She thinks differently, has unique likes and dislikes, has different needs, and responds to situations differently.

Describe one way you feel you have not been an understanding husband: _____

_____

Understanding that differences exist is a major part of understanding your wife. How you deal with these differences greatly influences the quality of your marriage.

This week take time to listen, to be respectful, to discuss plans and decisions, to compliment, to hear opinions, and to be patient with your wife. This is living in an understanding way, and God will bless your marriage for it.

Identify at least one way you will implement the concept of living with your wife in an understanding way this week:

_____

_____

How do you think God demonstrates relating to you in an understanding way?

_____

_____

_____

Finish the following prayer:

"Lord, help me to understand my wife by _____

_____

_____ *."*

DAY 3
Understand Differences Between You and Your Wife

Read Ephesians 4:1-6.

Before a man can live with his wife in an understanding way, he should realize why it is so difficult. Men and women are different from each other by design. Genesis 1:27 reads, "God created man in his own image, in the image of God he created him; male and female he created them." That God purposefully created people in two distinct sexes patterned after Himself is a great mystery. He desired that when a man and woman married, they should live as one, fulfilling His intentions. The differences between men and woman go beyond the physical distinctions.

Write down a few of the differences that you have observed.

MEN   WOMEN

_____   _____

_____   _____

_____   _____

These differences make up each gender's uniqueness. Our culture wants to remove those differences and promote a neutral gender that is neither masculine nor feminine, but that is not what God intended.

Often, our culture has stereotyped masculinity and femininity. Not all boys like contact sports and not all girls enjoy playing with dolls. Before we superimpose our definitions on others, we must examine where they came from. Are they based on our families of origin, background, influences, and role models, or are they biblical models? Write your definition of each:

To be masculine is to be _____

_____.

To be feminine is to be _____

_____.

Often, our preconceived notions set us up for false expectations in marriage. If a husband assumes all women like to cook, he may be distressed when his new bride wants to microwave a prepared dinner. In the same way, the bride may expect her husband to be a Mr. Fix-It, when he has no aptitude for mechanical things. Each married couple must be willing to learn about each other and make allowances for the differences that make them unique human beings. Learning about your wife, then, becomes your main task before God, just as you want her to learn about you.

List some of the ways you and your wife are different in the following categories:

	HUSBAND	WIFE
Personality	_____	_____
Temperament	_____	_____
Likes	_____	_____
Dislikes	_____	_____

In order to appreciate your wife's differences, you must see her as an equal—neither better than you nor worse than you— but certainly different from you. Our society would have you think that stripping gender makes us equal. In reality, culture is after sameness, not equality. God granted us equality as men and women created in His image, but that is not sameness.

Our equality is in Christ. Notice the unity and equality of men and women in Christ in Ephesians 4:1-6.
- one body
- one Spirit
- one hope
- one Lord
- one faith
- one baptism
- one God and Father

Recognizing the equality of men and women in Christ is vital to properly understanding Christianity. Understanding the roles and responsibilities that each has been given is equally important. The Christian husband's role in understanding his wife is twofold:

1. Recognize the differences in both personality and responsibility.
2. Understand her equality in the body of Christ.

Success in doing these things will assure your living with your wife in an understanding way. Offer God a prayer of thanksgiving for the unity in the body of Christ. Ask for understanding as you begin to define or as you clarify your role as a Christian husband.

DAY 4
Meet Her Needs

Read Proverbs 18:22.

As you live with your wife in an understanding way and you begin to recognize and affirm the differences between the two of you, you will grow closer together but not necessarily more alike. One of the ways you and your wife may continue to be different will be in your personal needs.

Chances are, you are fairly certain of your personal needs, but your wife's needs may be more confusing. Willard Harley, in his book *His Needs, Her Needs,* speaks directly about the needs of men and women. After counseling husbands and wives for over 30 years, he has developed a list of needs that, according to him, are typical of men and women.

TOP FIVE NEEDS OF MEN AND WOMEN

MEN	WOMEN
1. Sexual fulfillment	1. Affection
2. Recreational companionship	2. Conversation
3. An attractive spouse	3. Honesty and openness
4. Domestic support	4. Financial support
5. Admiration	5. Family commitment[1]

Your needs may or may not match Harley's list. People are unique and have varied needs and desires. Often men fail to understand the differences between sex and affection or problem-solving and conversation. Understanding how to give your wife what she needs rather than making her need what you can give is important to a successful marriage.

According to Harley, a man's top need is sexual fulfillment, while women desire affection.

How is being affectionate different from being sexual?

_____.

When you display affection to your wife, you are meeting a need within her. When you show her that you genuinely care about her needs and desires, you are living with her in an understanding way. Affection is more than the occasional "I love you." It is an openness and eagerness to be a part of your wife's life. You express affection by a tender touch, a hug, holding hands while you are walking, giving an affectionate pat or wink, stroking her hair, or admiring a new look.

A man's second need, according to Harley, is recreational companionship. Men like to spend time doing what they enjoy, which often means hanging out with the guys. Although hanging out typically doesn't include going shopping or watching a sad movie, men enjoy sharing their recreational lives with their wives.

What types of recreation do you enjoy with other men? _____

_____

What types of recreation could you invite your wife to participate in with you? _____

_____

While men desire recreational companionship, women desire conversation. Dr. Gary Rosberg said, "Women use conversation to enhance and expand relationships. Men use talk to convey solutions, thereby ending conversation."[2] How often do you try to solve rather than to listen to your wife's problems?

The difficulty for men is to simply listen to what their wives are thinking, feeling, and experiencing without judging or trying to solve the problem. A willingness to listen is more valuable to a woman than advice or a solution.

How well do you understand and meet your wife's needs? For each of the following areas, circle the word that best indicates how well you meet the needs:

I meet this need …

AFFECTION	Poorly	Well	Very well
CONVERSATION	Poorly	Well	Very well
HONESTY AND OPENNESS	Poorly	Well	Very well
FINANCIAL SUPPORT	Poorly	Well	Very well
FAMILY COMMITMENT	Poorly	Well	Very well

You may want to ask your wife to complete this activity as well. She can help you identify your strengths as well as weaknesses. Every man has the ability to meet the needs of his wife. With faith in God and an honest evaluation of yourself, you should be able to understand your wife's needs and begin to provide for those needs.

Write a prayer, asking God to grant you the ability to see your wife's needs and the strength to meet those needs.

_____

_____

DAY 5
Honor Your Wife

Read Galatians 3:26-29.

As we have discussed this week, living with your wife in an understanding way is crucial to a successful marriage. In day 2 you read 1 Peter 3:7 (NASB), "You husbands likewise, live with your wives in an understanding way, as with a weaker vessel, since she is a woman; and grant her honor as a fellow heir of the grace of life, so that your prayers may not be hindered." Today let's talk about what it means to honor your wife.

How do you honor someone? Finish the following statement:

To honor someone means to _____

_____.

We could define the word *honor* as a respect given to someone out of deep admiration. It is easy to see that we do not live in a world that knows how to honor women. Things such as crimes against women, spousal abuse, pornography, and male chauvinism indicate that our concept of honor is underdeveloped.

The Scriptures teach that men are to honor their wives as fellow heirs. Granting this kind of honor comes out of an attitude of respect. You will be unable to honor your wife if you have no respect for her. Place a check next to each item that you feel is respectful of your wife:

❑ yelling at your wife when you are angry
❑ lying to your wife
❑ being helpful
❑ remembering to do a favor for your wife
❑ being honest and open with your wife

❑ listening to your wife's concerns
❑ making your wife discipline the kids
❑ coming home late without calling
❑ providing for your wife's emotional needs
❑ forgetting important occasions

For a Christian, respect for women begins with Galatians 3:26-29. God sees everyone as equal heirs to the kingdom. Men need to learn how to see everyone the same way. God sees people as neither Jew nor Greek; neither slave nor free; neither male nor female; one in Christ; heirs according to the promise.

If you can begin to see your wife the way God sees her, then you can begin to grant her honor as a fellow heir of Christ. This mentality does not eliminate the roles that are distinct for each gender, but it does provide men with a proper understanding of women. For far too long, men have treated women as lesser creations. Women have revolted with the feminist movement. The result is a society in which many people are either trying to destroy the opposite sex or eliminate all differences.

Men and women have been given the salvation that everyone needs. There are no second-class citizens in God's kingdom. So why is there such a lack of respect for women? It begins with a son observing his father's actions. Men learn to treat women by seeing the way their fathers treated women. If a father has a poor view of women, he hands down that feeling.

Take a few moments to reflect on your father. Complete the following sentences:

My father treated my mother … _____

_____ .

My father expected my mother to … _____

_____ .

If you can begin to understand your father's attitude, you can begin to recognize why you do the things you do. Complete the following sentences about your own attitudes:

I treat my wife … _____

_____ .

I expect my wife to … _____

_____ .

The Christian husband has no room for arrogance or pride. He is to honor and respect his wife. First Peter 3:7 concludes, "so that your prayers may not be hindered." God will honor and answer your prayers only if you are willing to honor and respect your wife. Begin today to live with your wife in an understanding way, and learn to grant her honor.

Check the following ways you will seek to honor your wife this week:

❑ speak gently to her   ❑ show consideration for her feelings
❑ compliment her in front of others   ❑ pay attention when she speaks
❑ be courteous (open doors, pull out her chair)   ❑ serve her in some practical way
❑ demand respect for her from the children

Pray this prayer: *"Lord, as You love me, help me to love my wife. Help me to understand her needs and give me the strength to meet them. As we strive to meld Your image in us, give us Your Holy Spirit to lead us. Thank You for the gift of my wife. Help me to honor her all the days of my life. Amen."*

WEEK 3

ANCHORING YOUR
FAMILY CHAIN

VIEWER GUIDE

Families drift because they lack male _____.

If you don't have [a godly family heritage], then you _____ it.

The great thing about coming to know Christ—you can put a _____ _____ in your family chain.

You stop the drifting in a family when a man gets anchored on _____ _____.

There is a difference between *wisdom* and *obedience*. Wisdom is having great _____ into the truth.

Just because you have wisdom doesn't insure that you'll obey the _____.

Our kids are becoming _____ _____ as to what's right and what's wrong.

How do you help your kids to make it through the moral fog?

By cutting a swath of _____ to Jesus Christ and His Word.

As you follow Christ, you cut a path of clarity that they can then step through and _____ in your footsteps.

God wants our hearts to be so fully His in _____ that as we walk with Him, our leadership and our

example will _____ and _____ our families for the next 100 years.

You should be a legend in your family in 100 years because of your _____ to your wife and your

family and, most of all, your love for Jesus Christ. You ought to be an _____.

You lead a family for 100 years by following Jesus Christ today with your _____ _____.

DAY 1
The Rising Tide

Read Matthew 13:11-17.

An incredible change has occurred in American families over the past one hundred years. We have experienced a great shifting in our foundations. With the rise in marital problems and subsequent divorce, many families no longer have a solid foundation on which to stand. Children have fathers who live in one city and mothers who live in another. Families are being separated geographically, emotionally, and spiritually.

Even when the father is in the home, we are a country full of "drifting families." What are drifting families like?
- Drifting families lack leadership.
- Drifting families lack direction.
- Drifting families lack strategy.
- Drifting families lack vision.

These families are caught in a rising tide and are heading for destruction. They are adrift in an immoral and wicked sea. What makes a family drift? It is a family that has lost its anchor.

The anchor of a family is Christ. God has given the father the responsibility for keeping his family firmly anchored in Christ. When the father leaves, abuses, or neglects his wife and children, the family begins to drift.

How about your family? Is it in danger of drifting? Evaluate your family by the criteria listed above. Place a check under the appropriate column.

	TRUE OF MY FAMILY	NOT TRUE OF MY FAMILY
Drifting families lack leadership.	❑	❑
Drifting families lack direction.	❑	❑
Drifting families lack strategy.	❑	❑
Drifting families lack vision.	❑	❑

Is your family in danger of drifting? Are you anchoring your family in Christ? Do you provide leadership in taking your family to church, leading family devotions, being an example in prayer and Bible study, and practicing servant leadership in the home, church, and community?

Proverbs 20:7 says, "The righteous man leads a blameless life, blessed are his children after him." We cannot expect others to supply the anchor our families need. It is our responsibility. It is our calling.

The passage from Matthew 13 is a good description of the world today. All around us, we can see and hear the truth about God, yet many people are deaf and blind to the truth. So many people have hardened their hearts toward God that they are unable to know and to do what is right.

In Matthew 13:11, who did Jesus say had been given "knowledge of the secrets of the kingdom of heaven"?
(check one)
❑ the religious leaders of His day
❑ the large crowds who had gathered to hear Him speak
❑ His disciples

How about you? If you claim Jesus as your Lord and Savior and have promised to obey Him as your Master, you have been given the knowledge of the secrets of the kingdom of heaven (Matt. 13:11). Are you letting yourself go blind and deaf, or are you striving to know and live the truth? God wants you to anchor your family in His Word and to save them from drifting.

Is it possible that your family is drifting and you are not aware? We sometimes think we have anchored our families in Christ when in fact we are adrift ourselves. Here are some "anchors" that hold families together in the short term. Answer the following questions by circling yes or no.

- Is your family anchored with money?   Yes   No

- Is your family anchored with fun vacations?   Yes   No

- Is your family anchored by school and homework?   Yes   No

- Is your family anchored with athletics?   Yes   No

- Is your family anchored with recreation?   Yes   No

- Is your family anchored with Christ?   Yes   No

We can try to anchor our families with many things. Money, entertainment, and sports can all offer a certain amount of security, but if your family is not grounded in the faith, you are drifting in this world. Jesus is the only One who can offer you a true anchor. Your family needs you to hold fast to Christ.

Write a brief prayer, asking God to show you what your anchors are. Ask Him to give you the strength and wisdom to be anchored in Christ.

_____

_____

DAY 2
The Anchor

Read Deuteronomy 6:1-9.

Have you ever thought about your heritage? What or who in your past has helped define who you are today? *Webster's Dictionary* defines *heritage* as "something possessed as a result of one's natural situation or birth." Your heritage is the inheritance, whether good or bad, that you received at your birth.

The one unchangeable quality about your heritage is that you were not able to choose it. It was passed down to you from your parents who received it from their parents. It is as much a part of you as the color of your eyes. You will pass a heritage to your children and to their children as well. What is your heritage?

Think about your parents. Consider all of the things, both material and immaterial, they have given to you. Circle the items below that you have received as a part of your heritage:

wealth	confidence	truthfulness
bad temper	alcoholism	respect for others
athletic ability	abusive tendencies	family name
faith	good looks	love for God

your additions to the list: _____

Many more categories could be included in this list. The important thing is to realize what you have been given. More importantly, you need to realize what you will be passing on as a heritage for your children.

In day 1 we talked about drifting families—also a part of many men's heritage. This type of family will unfortunately be passed on to many children. The question is, how do we keep our families from drifting? How can we give them a heritage that is strong? The answer is Christ.

A man stops the drifting in a family when he gets anchored in Jesus Christ. When Christ is that anchor, the family has vision, discernment, leadership, and strategy. The family has a purpose and is not simply adrift in the world.

What does it mean to anchor your family in Christ? Deuteronomy 6:5 says, "Love the Lord your God with all your heart and with all your soul and with all your strength." This is how you anchor your family in Jesus. Your loving God and obeying what He says is the most important heritage you can give your family.

Moses says in verse 7, "Impress [God's commandments] on your children." You are to make an impression on your children by modeling and teaching obedience to God's commands. You should do this:
- when you sit at home
- when you walk along the road
- when you lie down
- when you rise up

Everything you do is part of the heritage you give to your family. If you have anchored yourself and your family in Christ, you are showing your children how to love God. God will bless you for it.

You teach your children many things every day, whether or not you are aware of it. Much of what they know about life they have learned from you. Describe a way you can teach your children God's commands as you:

drive them to school or activities _____

_____

work with them around the house or in the yard _____

_____

If you are anchoring yourself in Christ, your list will include talking with them about such subjects as how to pray, how to be honest, and how to respect their mother. Your family is your greatest responsibility. Give them a godly heritage that they one day will be able to pass on to their children.

A family that is anchored in Christ and His Word is not easily set adrift by the enemy. Are you anchored in Jesus? Is your family drifting, or are you holding them tightly as Jesus holds you? Write a brief prayer, asking God for wisdom in giving your family a heritage that is worthwhile and lasting.

_____

_____

_____

_____

DAY 3
The Charge

Read 1 Timothy 3:1-13.

We live in an interesting age. Much confusion exists about roles within society. Many men have lost their identity and are uncertain about how or when to act. The search for identity can be a difficult task.

Our homes and churches deal with this same confusion. People are no longer certain who should or should not be ministering or leading. For men especially, old models of leadership are being dismantled and are being replaced by new, more politically-correct models. The times are changing.

However, several things do not change:
• God does not change.
• God's Word does not change.
• Our basic responsibilities do not change.

God has given us His Word and Spirit to guide us into the truth. His Word clearly defines the type of man God is looking for to serve in His church, in the family, and in the world. This responsibility does not discount women's gifts or ministries, but it does make a man's place within the home and church unique.

Today the church is influenced by the world rather than influencing the world. God has called men to be godly leaders, and it is up to men to decide whether they take up their responsibilities. Although the 1 Timothy passage we read today concerns the qualities of the overseers (pastors) and deacons of the early church, these same qualities should be true for every godly man.

What, then, should a man be like if he is to be a godly leader? Read verses 1-7 again and write in the following spaces the qualities of spiritual leaders:

above _____,

the husband of but _____ wife,

temperate, self-controlled, respectable, hospitable, able to teach,

not given to _____,

not violent but _____,

not quarrelsome, not a lover of _____,

manage his own family _____, not a recent _____, and

have a good _____.

Leadership is a high calling. A true leader does not simply delegate assignments and give discipline—a true leader leads by example. Certainly, everyone should strive to gain the qualities in 1 Timothy 3, but leaders in particular should work diligently to develop these qualities. For men who want to anchor their families in Christ, these qualities are essential. Ask yourself...

- How am I being a leader in my family?
- How am I being a leader in my church?

Look back at the list of leadership qualities in 1 Timothy 3. How strong are you in each item? In the boxes below, indicate your strengths or weaknesses by placing each quality in the appropriate box. For example, if you are strong in self-control, write it in the "Excellent" box.

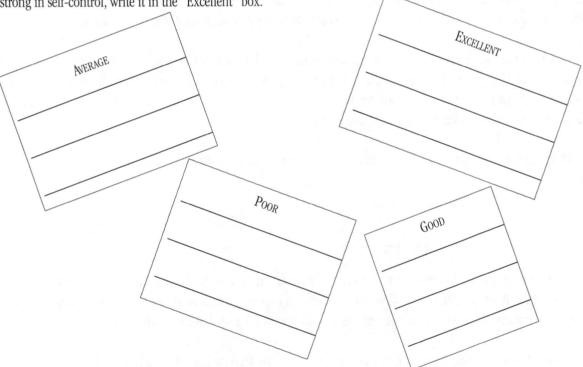

It is good to recognize your leadership strengths as well as your weaknesses. Realize that being what God called you to be is going to be a lifelong process. With His help, you can do all things. Write a short prayer, asking God to help you maintain your strengths and to help you improve your weaknesses:

_____

_____

DAY 4
Listening and Doing

Read James 1:19-27.

Imagine that you have been given the opportunity to ask God for anything you want and He will give it to you. Of all the things for which you could ask, what do you want most of all? Write down your answer.

_____

Many different requests may have run through your mind. Perhaps you would ask for health, happiness, money, or fame. Perhaps you would ask to be the greatest evangelist ever or to have the power to heal. You could want a lot of things.

One person, in fact, was given this opportunity. Instead of money, fame, or power, Solomon, the son of King David, asked God for wisdom. God granted him wisdom that will never be equaled. Unfortunately for Solomon, he did not also receive the ability to obey what he knew was right. He knew the truth, but he didn't always follow it. James 1:22 says, "Do not merely listen to the word, and so deceive yourselves. Do what it says."

How would you explain to one of your children the difference between listening and obeying?

_____

_____

A man who listens to God and then does what he is told is a man on the right track toward being anchored in Christ. Wisdom and obedience are different. Wisdom is having insight into the truth, which often comes from listening to God through His written and spoken Word. Obedience is the willingness to do what one knows is right.

Our world is full of enemies who try to get us to forget what we have been taught—to simply blend in. When they were entering the promised land, the Israelites were surrounded by pagans who did not want them to do what they had been taught. God had given the Israelites specific instructions concerning the promised land. It was their duty to carry them out.

Speaking to the men of Israel, Moses said, "Now this is the commandment, the statutes and the judgments which the Lord your God has commanded me to teach you, that you might do them" (Deut. 6:1, NASB). The important part was that the men were to do what they had been taught. Learning the commandments, statutes, and judgments was not enough. To have success, they needed to put into action the laws they had been taught.

How important is it to do what you have been taught?
- When you drive a car, do you obey the traffic signals? ☐ Yes ☐ No
- When you play a sport, do you observe the rules? ☐ Yes ☐ No
- As a member of society, do you follow the laws? ☐ Yes ☐ No

Failure to do what you were taught in these situations could lead to personal harm, injury to others, or punishment by the authorities. How much more important is it that we obey the rules our Heavenly Father has given us? God has shown us how to live and to live more abundantly. If we choose to ignore what He has taught us, we are choosing a way of life that will end in death. There is no "make it up as you go" in Christianity.

Solomon was the wisest man to ever live, but he chose to harden his heart toward God. As a result, the end of his life was dismal and without the joy of the Lord. Wisdom means learning to live in harmony with the laws of God.

Below are several characteristics from James 1:19-27 that Christians should try to attain. Place an X on the line indicating how well you feel you are practicing each virtue.

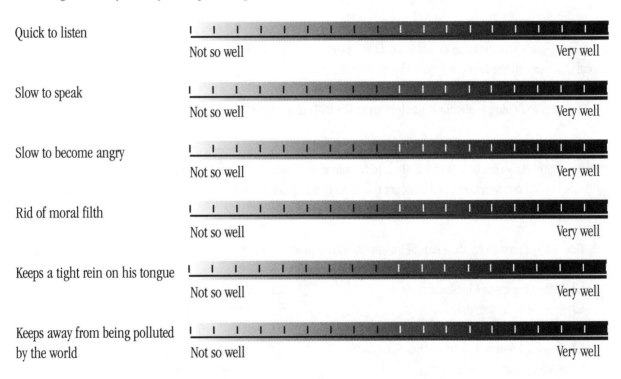

Quick to listen — Not so well / Very well

Slow to speak — Not so well / Very well

Slow to become angry — Not so well / Very well

Rid of moral filth — Not so well / Very well

Keeps a tight rein on his tongue — Not so well / Very well

Keeps away from being polluted by the world — Not so well / Very well

The easy part of the spiritual life is knowing what to do. The difficulty lies in doing what one knows. God wants you to be a doer of His Word and not a hearer only. (See Jas. 1:22.) Anchor yourself in His Word, and let His Word transform your actions in yourself, your home, your church, and your world.

Complete the following prayer, asking for God's help in doing what is right and in persevering to the end:

"Lord, help me be a doer of Your Word by _____

_____. "

DAY 5
The Reward

Read Deuteronomy 7:8-13.

Our country has undergone many amazing changes over the last one hundred years. Changes such as automobiles, nuclear power, space exploration, genetic engineering, and cures for hundreds of diseases have changed the world that our grandparents and great-grandparents knew. We can hardly imagine what the 21st century will bring.

Our country has undergone some fairly dramatic moral changes as well. The prevalence of homosexuality, abortion, sexual immorality, and domestic violence are indications of the moral degeneration that we as a nation are experiencing. What moral changes will the next one hundred years bring?
- How are you preparing yourself spiritually for the future?
- What are you doing to anchor your children in the faith of their fathers?

God has a mandate for our lives. His mandate is that our hearts be so fully obedient to Him that, as we walk with Him, our leadership and our example will glorify Him. In Scripture God continually speaks about generations. He is concerned that we think beyond our own needs and embrace the needs of the generations that will follow us. We need to think about leading and anchoring our families for the next one hundred years.

How do you prepare for the needs of the generations that will follow you? In the following list, check each item that you feel will help prepare your children to be Christlike.
- ❏ buying expensive Christmas presents
- ❏ praying with them daily
- ❏ making sure they brush their teeth
- ❏ showing them how to treat strangers
- ❏ teaching them to repair things
- ❏ taking them to church regularly
- ❏ making sure they have a nutritious diet
- ❏ reading the Bible with them often
- ❏ attending their athletic events
- ❏ attending their recitals and performances

All too often, men take care of their children's physical needs while they overlook their spiritual needs entirely. As the one charged with anchoring your family, it is your responsibility to provide spiritual instruction and example to your children. God has called you to this position, and He expects you to fulfill it.

When a person continually saves a small amount of money and earns a modest interest on that money, eventually it will compound into a large sum. The guiding principle behind this theory is the continual discipline of saving. Eventually, all your sacrifice will pay off.

This same theory applies to your family. Every time a man walks in obedience to Christ, lives with his wife in an understanding way, helps a stranger, or teaches his children to love the Lord, he is making a deposit. God, in turn, is going to repay him with compound interest.

Deuteronomy 7:9 says, "Know therefore that the Lord your God is God; he is the faithful God, keeping his covenant of love to a thousand generations of those who love him and keep his commands" (NIV). How has God been covenantally faithful to you? List several ways:

_____

_____

_____

_____

We are not simply raising children; we are raising child-raisers. To anchor your family chain, you know and obey God's Word, and you raise children who will desire to follow your example.

Many of us were blessed with Christian fathers and grandfathers. They are good examples of what it means to anchor your family in Christ. In the following space, write your Christian family tree. Begin by writing the name of the earliest Christian you can recall in your family. Continue with their children and grandchildren until you arrive at yourself. If this does not apply to you, make yours look toward the future. Just as my grandfather did, you can decide to start this tree with yourself.

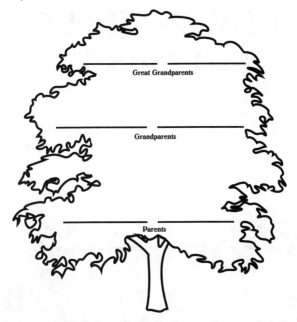

God is the God of the covenant who passes on His blessing to a thousand generations. Pray that God, in His mercy, may preserve our families as we strive to anchor them in Christ.

WEEK 4

THE SEVEN STEPS OF FATHERING

VIEWER GUIDE

Fathers are to:

1. _____

     _____ is a curse. It robs a man of the leadership in his home.

     The fear of the Lord is the beginning of _____.

     Look for teachable situations in life and _____.

     Be a man who

       • _____ Jesus Christ.

       • _____ Scriptures.

       • _____ the Scriptures to life.

2. teach

3. _____

4. _____

5. be _____

6. be _____

7. be _____

DAY 1
A Changing Role

Read Deuteronomy 6:1-7.

A father's tasks are numerous and sometimes quite difficult. Fathering requires tremendous attention, discipline, and self-lessness. Our culture promotes and embraces many ideas and priorities that only make fathering more difficult. In fact, being a father becomes increasingly difficult every day.

In America, the role and responsibility of fathers has changed over the years. We can look back through history to discover how and why these changes began. The industrial revolution was a pivotal time in the history of families. This revolution changed our culture drastically. Few elements of society were affected more than the role of fathers.

If you look at life before the industrial revolution, you will notice several characteristics:
- Society was mainly rural.
- Fathers worked primarily at the home.
- Fathers apprenticed their sons.
- Mothers apprenticed their daughters.
- The home was the center of life.

After the industrial revolution, people's roles changed and responsibilities were switched. After the industrial revolution:
- Society was mainly urban.
- Fathers worked primarily away from the home.
- Sons and daughters were raised mainly by mothers.
- A large amount of family time was taken away.

I believe that another key change resulted. A general loss of personal identity and self-worth settled on the male population. One of the key effects of the industrial revolution impacted the family and children. As men were taken out of the home, they were no longer so directly involved in training their sons. As a result, when the men left to work in factories, family difficulty, juvenile delinquency, and despair came in.

What is our nation's situation today? Today most men and women work outside the home. As a result, "care-givers" rather than parents raise many children. With the high divorce rate, many children do not have proper role models. The role of the father is more difficult than ever because he has less time with his family. However, his role remains crucial.

We began this week by reading Deuteronomy 6:1-7. During the week, we will expound on the seven techniques found in Deuteronomy 6.

1. Fathers are to initiate action.
2. Fathers are to teach.
3. Fathers are to discipline.
4. Fathers are to communicate.
5. Fathers are to be available.
6. Fathers are to be aware.
7. Fathers are to be involved.

As you look at this list, you may feel discouraged or overwhelmed. We must understand the reality of the problems that most fathers face in fulfilling these responsibilities. Equally important, we must find ways to deal with these problems and become active fathers.

Understanding your strengths and weaknesses will allow you to concentrate on improvements you need to make. All fathers are strong in some areas and weak in others. You may be strong in the ability to communicate, but weak on availability or discipline. The goal of this week is to learn how to make improvements in your fathering skills.

What is your greatest strength as a father? _____

Why? _____

What is your weakness? _____

Why? _____

As a father, you have an enormous responsibility. You must raise children in a world that is often hostile and usually cruel. Deuteronomy 6 is a fundamental chapter for fathers who want to be effective. As we look through this passage this week, pray that God will help you to be a doer of His Word and not a hearer only. Write a brief prayer, asking for God's wisdom in helping you incorporate His Word into your life.

_____

_____

_____

_____

DAY 2
Initiate Action

Read Proverbs 4.

In Deuteronomy 6:1 we read, "these are the commandments, decrees and laws the Lord your God directed me to teach you to observe in the land that you are crossing the Jordan to possess." The first step to fathering is to take the initiative. God has put on the father the responsibility of teaching children. One of the temptations of manhood and of being a father is falling into passivity.

What do you think a passive man looks and acts like? Complete the following sentences contrasting the two:

A passive man is _____

_____

An active man is _____

_____

God calls fathers to be active when it comes to raising their children. Too many men believe that the kids are the wife's responsibility, and they take a passive role in teaching, disciplining, and mentoring. How well do you initiate action in these three areas? On the following line, place an X indicating where your initiative lies:

Passive   Active

Many men have high-pressure jobs that require them to make tough decisions, manage others, or mentor younger professionals as they enter the working world. Yet, these same men, when they come home at night, lose all sense of leadership for their children. They provide "fathering" to everyone except their own children. They have a misplaced sense of duty.

When this happens, a family is in trouble. Someone must take on the role of leader. If the father is unwilling, often the mother is left to pick up the slack. Passivity robs the man of the leadership of his home. The enemy wants to neutralize men. When men are passive, they are helping the enemy.
- A passive man waits for something to go wrong.
- An active man prepares for difficulty and handles situations efficiently on the front end.

In today's world, children face many alarming and dangerous situations. How do you think both an active and a passive father would act in the following situations?

- In response to the pressure to do drugs:

a passive father would _____

an active father would _____

- To prepare his children to face sexual temptation:

a passive father would _____

an active father would _____

- To train his children to deal with the violence in today's society:

a passive father would _____

an active father would _____

- To help his children choose what they will believe about God:

a passive father would _____

an active father would _____

Active fathering requires work. All the factors of fathering in Deuteronomy 6 revolve around the father's initiative. That means you can't sit back and wait for something to happen before you decide what to do. It means you give your children a moral base to stand on. You teach them how to deal with temptation and how to control their anger. Being an active father means you lead your family on paths of righteousness. Proverbs 4 is a wonderful exhortation about fathering. If you as a father can maintain an attitude of anticipating and heading off problems, you will help your children embrace a godly life.

"Lay hold of my words with all your heart; keep my commands and you will live" (Prov. 4:4).

God desires that you lead your children just as He leads us as our Heavenly Father. The first step is to initiate action. Write a brief prayer, asking God to help you take the first step in being a godly father.

_____

_____

_____

DAY 3
Teach Your Children

Read Proverbs 22:6.

When a father takes an active role in the life of his children, he will find that his main task is to teach. All of life is an education, and you must take the lead role in what your children are taught. Teaching is done through actions more than words. You will teach your children by what you do or by what you don't do every day of their lives. Your children will remember your example long after they forget your words.

In our culture, ideals and morals have changed so drastically that you must make every effort to teach your children well. What are some of the lessons you feel are important for your children to learn from you?

❑ "An honest day's work for an honest day's pay."   ❑ "A man's word is his law.:"
❑ "A penny saved is a penny earned."   ❑ "A lie will always find you out."
❑ "It's what's on the inside that counts, not what's on the outside."
❑ other _____

How do you teach your children?

• Do you only tell them what to do?
• Do you show them by example?
• Do you simply hope for the best?
• Do you set standards and equip your children with the tools to meet them?

Seven percent of what any person learns is learned through verbal communication. The remainder is learned through non-verbal communication or by example. As a teacher, your first priority is to practice what you preach. Your children will follow your example regardless of what you say. The habits that you teach them now will manifest themselves for the rest of their lives. Those habits can be good or bad.

Write down a few things your children have learned from your example:

GOOD HABITS   BAD HABITS

_____   _____

_____   _____

_____   _____

Many people wonder why our nation is in such turmoil. A nation is only as strong as the families that live in it. Our country is in trouble because we have too many fathers who fail to teach their children values. Too many fathers let their children wander into a world that will devour them. We are reaping the consequences of weak fathering. Another word for *fathering* is *discipleship*. Discipleship can only take place when you are with your children. Christ Himself discipled people by being with them. This is one of the keys to effective teaching.

Proverbs 22:6 says, "Train a child in the way he should go, and when he is old he will not turn from it." Teaching your child is giving them that foundation by which they can succeed in life. It is giving them a heritage and reason for living in a world that is full of people who feel disconnected and meaningless.

In Deuteronomy 6 we read that men were to teach their sons and grandsons the fear of the Lord. Psalm 111:10 says, "The fear of the Lord is the beginning of wisdom." If you are to raise godly children, they must learn a proper respect and admiration for God. This begins with proper respect and admiration for you. Is anything blocking that from occurring? Seek counsel from your wife, Sunday School teacher, pastor, or friend. Ask for their honest feedback.

How much time do you spend with your children? Fill in the following spaces with the time you have spent together and what you have done with your children over the last three days:

Day #1: Time spent _____

Activities: _____

_____

Day #2: Time spent _____

Activities: _____

_____

Day #3: Time spent _____

Activities: _____

_____

Do you see both quality and quantity of time you are spending with your kids? The more time you spend with your children, the more influence you will have and the more you can teach them. Your quantity of time will determine your quality of time.

Complete the following prayer: *Father, help me to teach my children* _____

_____.

DAY 4
Discipline Your Children

Read Proverbs 22:15.

A third trait of biblical fathering appears in Deuteronomy 6. Fathers are not only to initiate and teach, they are to discipline. Verse 2 says, "so that you, your children and their children after them may fear the Lord." Your duty is to raise children who appreciate what it means to fear the Lord. If you are successful, they will in turn raise children who fear the Lord.

Why is a father's discipline essential? If a child does not first learn the fear of a father, a child will not learn the fear of the Lord. To properly fear someone does not mean that you are afraid they will hurt you. A child who properly fears his father understands that wrongdoing results in punishment. The goal is to instill respect for authority and accountability for personal actions.

In *Standing Tall* the point is made that *strict* is an unpopular word today, yet it is a necessary word. We have few fathers in this nation who know how to be strict–in the best sense of the term. We have fathers who are more interested in being popular with their kids than they are in being respected by their kids. And there lies our problem (*Standing Tall*, 51).

How do you feel about the statement that *strict* is an unpopular word?

❏ strongly disagree   ❏ disagree   ❏ agree   ❏ strongly agree

Why? _____

_____

In *You and Your Child,* Chuck Swindoll discusses the Houston Police Department's efforts to encourage parental guidance. The department circulated a pamphlet entitled "Twelve Rules for Raising Delinquent Children." The rules are as follows:
1. Begin with infancy to give the child everything he wants. In this way he will grow up to believe the world owes him a living.
2. When he picks up bad words, laugh at him. This will make him think he's cute.
3. Never give him any spiritual training. Wait until he is twenty-one and then let "him decide for himself."
4. Avoid the use of *wrong*. He may develop a guilt complex. This will condition him to believe later, when he is arrested for stealing a car, that society is against him and he is being persecuted.
5. Pick up everything he leaves lying around. Do everything for him so that he will be experienced in throwing all responsibility on others.

6. Let him read any printed matter he can get his hands on. Be careful that the silverware and drinking glasses are sterilized, but let his mind feast on garbage.

7. Quarrel frequently in the presence of your children. In this way they won't be so shocked when the home is broken up later.

8. Give the child all the spending money he wants. Never let him earn his own.

9. Satisfy his every craving for food, drink, and comfort. See that his every sensual desire is gratified.

10. Take his part against neighbors, teachers, and policemen. They are all prejudiced against your child.

11. When he gets into trouble, apologize for yourself by saying, "I could never do anything with him."

12. Prepare for a life of grief. You will be likely to have it (*Standing Tall,* 51).

Obviously the police department is trying to help parents understand their role in their child's behavior. As the father, it is your responsibility to maintain discipline in your home. Too often, men leave all the discipline to their wives. The result is a child's lack of respect for the father. The mother's role is also confused, and the family is in chaos.

Proverbs 22:15 says, "Folly is bound up in the heart of a child, but the rod of discipline will drive it far from him." The "rod of discipline" is that action from the parent that provides consequences for a child's actions. If a parent has an attitude of love and self-control, those consequences will be effective but not harmful.

The concept of discipline has been undermined today because too many people have taken discipline to the extreme of abuse. Discipline is not abuse but rather the establishment of boundaries and consequences. There is a difference between discipline and abuse.

	DISCIPLINE	ABUSE
The intent:	Training: to correct problem behavior	Violence: intent to injure
The attitude:	Love and concern	Anger and malice
The effect:	Behavioral correction	Emotional/physical injury

The responsibility of a father is to correct the children, not injure them. As a Christian, it is your responsibility to raise children in the fear of the Lord. It is the greatest gift that you as a parent can give them.

Check ways you seek to discipline your children. Underline ways you want to add to your list of possibilities.

❑ time-out chair location
❑ repaying or replacing item lost or broken
❑ written or oral apology
❑ other _____

❑ taking away privileges, such as phone or computer
❑ having to miss a sporting or recreational outing
❑ talk about the offense; explain consequences; pray together

Write a brief prayer, asking God for guidance as you discipline your children.

_____

_____

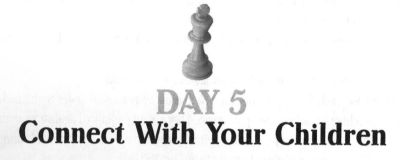

DAY 5
Connect With Your Children

Read 3 John 4.

What is your greatest joy? _____

How does it match the words of 3 John 4? (circle one)   exactly   somewhat   not at all

Today we will discuss the final four steps of fathering found in Deuteronomy 6. These four can be summed up in the word *connect*.

- Fathers are to communicate.
- Fathers are to be available.
- Fathers are to be aware.
- Fathers are to be involved.

Fathers are to communicate. Deuteronomy 6:7 says, "Impress them on your children. Talk about them when you sit at home and when you walk along the road, when you lie down and when you get up." Fathers are to communicate the Word of God to their children whenever possible. This doesn't mean that you are a walking seminary, but it does mean that your words, attitudes, and actions reflect Christ.

Communicating with your children can be a daunting task. Often we find it easier to talk *to* them, rather than *with* them. Talking *to* them may be interpreted as preaching or nagging, and they may tune you out. Talking *with* them is the work of entering into their lives. It communicates caring and concern. It involves knowing the world in which your child lives.

Evaluate your level of communication by circling the ways your children would describe your messages to them:

preaching   caring   nagging   loving   judging

belittling   encouraging   griping   advising   helping

Fathers are to be available. Availability is a rare commodity for most men. We have work obligations that demand much of our time and attention. We have personal interests that we indulge. Our wives often feel they have to compete for our time. Unfortunately, our children are the ones usually left out of the picture.

To father your children properly, you must make time to be available to them. They must know that they are a priority in your life, or they will look for the attention they need elsewhere.

Both sons and daughters need your time. Both have special needs that only you can meet. Use the following spaces to write some specific ways you can make time to be available to your children:

To be available to my children, I will _____

_____.

Fathers are to be aware. Awareness requires focus, undivided attention. In this age of cell phones, beepers, and wireless Internet, it is increasingly difficult for a father to leave work at the office. When you are spending time with the children, focus your attention on them. To really be aware, you must take precautions against distractions.

What is your biggest distraction while with your children? _____

Make a commitment to be focused on your children when you spend time with them. Think of several ways of avoiding distraction when you are with them:

I can stay focused on my children by _____

_____.

Fathers are to be involved. Involvement with your children may require a sacrifice of your time. If you want to teach and mentor your children, you must be involved in their lives. Here are some suggestions:
- Attend their sporting events.
- Go to their plays or recitals.
- Encourage them to tell you about their day.
- Take them out individually to show them special attention.
- Encourage and support them in their interests.
- Eat meals together.
- Do homework together.

Involvement also includes knowing what they are reading, watching, and hearing. Can you name your children's favorite television show, radio station, movie star, musician, or sports celebrity? If not, find out by asking questions that reflect interest, not judging. If something you hear from them displeases you, gently lead them to other activities or interests.

The reward for this kind of fathering is found in 3 John 4: "I have no greater joy than to hear that my children are walking in the truth." A father's job well done is a child's life well lived.

Write a prayer, asking for God's help as you make these commitments. _____

_____.

WEEK 5

RAISING MASCULINE SONS AND FEMININE DAUGHTERS

VIEWER GUIDE

We are raising children in a time of tremendous _____ _____.

A man and his son—the best place to start is to have a _____ _____.

A masculine man is going to bring the appropriate _____ to the appropriate _____.

Jesus could be aggressive, bold, courageous, kind, gentle, at any given moment, depending on what the situation

called for. That's what it means to be a _____ man.

Men are to love their wives in such a way that they would do anything to protect their wives and to achieve the best

for their wives. Jesus is the model. Jesus was willing to _____ for the church. Jesus was willing to

_____ _____ for the church.

Every Scripture that instructs a man on how to treat, honor, and respect his wife

can also be applied to his _____.

Your daughter will know what kind of guy is _____ by watching your example.

You can help your daughter have a _____ _____ by showing her what it means to be a godly man.

Every family needs

1. _____.

2. _____.

_____ are to be the primary providers.

_____ are to be the primary caregivers.

DAY 1
Your Child's Development

Read Psalm 127:3-5.

This week we will be discussing the issue of raising masculine sons and feminine daughters. This topic may seem obvious to you, but because the values of our society are so twisted, we must keep biblical standards before our children. We have already discussed what it means to be made in the image of God. We can say with certainty:

- God created men to be masculine.
- God created women to be feminine.
- God approves of these distinctions.

In our culture, we have seen a dramatic rise in the confusion of gender roles and identity. Men are increasingly becoming feminized. Women are becoming more masculine. In this confusion, our children are left with little understanding of who they are or who they will become.

Today we are going to look at the phases of child development and how each phase determines the child's identity. These phases are generally true with children. You will have to relate these general stages of development to your own experience and that of your children.

Phase #1   Paternal Differentiation Stage (Ages 1-5)

At this stage, the child develops sex-role orientation that answers the question, "What am I?" The father is the primary source of gender-role differentiation. The psychologist Sueann Robinson Ambrom, in *Child Development,* writes, "In gender-role development the evidence points to fathers as having an important influence not only in fostering a male self concept in boys, but femininity in girls. Mothers do contribute to their daughters' adoption of the feminine role, but have little influence on the masculinity of their sons."[1] As a father, you need to be aware of the crucial role you play in your child's development of self.

Phase #2   The Heterosexual Stage (Ages 6-8)

At this stage, the child establishes sex-role preference that answers the question, "What do I want to be?" If the father is fulfilled in his gender role, the sons will choose to be like him. If the father is an effective husband and the wife is fulfilled, the daughters will model her behavior.

Phase #3   The Modeling Stage (Ages 9-11)

In the Modeling Stage, the child establishes sex-role adoption that answers the question, "How do I act?" If the parents are fulfilled in their respective gender roles, the sons will absorb the masculinity of their fathers and the daughters will absorb their mother's femininity. In this stage, the children are watching to see who does what. They will act in much the same way when they are adults.

Phase #4   The Preparation Stage (Ages 12-marriage)

At this stage, the young adult establishes sex-role confirmation that answers the question, "How am I doing?" Both boys and girls will relate to the opposite sex the way dad related to mom. The importance of the role of the father cannot be understated here. Your sons are going to relate to their wives the same way you relate to your wife. Your daughters will seek a relationship that resembles that of you and your wife. Whether it is good or bad, your marriage is going to be a template for your children.

In today's society, many men are confused as to what their roles are. In Scripture, you will find a perfect example of the way a man should live. That example is Jesus Christ. Though Jesus was neither a husband or father, both men and women will find success as a mates and parents as they develop the character traits He displayed.

What are some character traits you see in Jesus that could make you a better father?

_____

_____

Look again at Psalm 127. What principle from the Psalm would you like to instill in your child or children?

_____

_____

What character traits do you need to pray for in your children's lives at their present stage of development?

_____

_____

Children are a blessing from the Lord. Fathering today is difficult and demanding. Using the wisdom God has given you, the discipline you have learned, and the help of the Holy Spirit, you will be able to raise godly children who will benefit the world for generations to come.

DAY 2
A Father and His Son (Part 1)

Read Romans 12:9-21.

John Piper said, "The tendency today is to stress the equality of men and women by minimizing the unique significance of maleness and femaleness. It is taking a tremendous toll on generations of young men and women who do not know what it means to be a man or a woman" (*Point Man,* 201). In our modern environment of gender confusion, Christian fathers and mothers have a unique opportunity to model the best of maleness and femaleness. If you have a marriage that follows the concepts of the Word of God, then you will teach both your sons and daughters how to express a balanced Christian character through the uniqueness of their masculinity or femininity.

In Paul's wonderful statement of Christlike character, he balanced the so-called "soft" issues like love with the more assertive traits like zeal. What character traits in Roman's 12:9-21 do you find most easily expressed?

_____

Which do you find most difficult?

_____

In the following section, circle the characteristics that you closely relate to Christianity:

Gentle   Loving   Passionate   Kind   Zealous

Courageous   Just   Bold   Humble   Merciful

Fervent   Devoted   Peaceful   Hospitable

All of these characteristics are Christian qualities. Often, we think of certain characteristics as being more Christian than others, when the real issue is how they are exercised. A man can be courageous and bold in witnessing for the Lord as well as in protecting his family from danger.

Your perception of what is Christlike behavior was probably formed by the society in which you grew up and now live. In modern Western society, where desk work has replaced hard physical labor for most breadwinners, the more rugged and adventuresome masculine traits are relegated to sports and the military.

We tend to take certain Christian traits such as gentleness, kindness, and compassion, and elevate them as primary traits. The truth is that all the Christian traits are desirable. Using them appropriately is the key. Paul prayed for "fearlessness" in Ephesians 6:19-20, and Jude prayed for men to "contend for the faith" (Jude 3).

In each of the examples below choose a word from the following list of character traits that you think is an appropriate expression of Christian masculinity: kind, gentle, courageous, steadfast, bold, just, merciful, forgiving.

_____ 1. Your son wants to go to an R-rated movie.
_____ 2. Your daughter wants to wear clothing that is sexually stimulating.
_____ 3. Your wife is feeling blue and wants to be comforted.
_____ 4. Your 16-year-old was in a car accident that was not his or her fault.

The enemy has neutralized men by taking away their roles and identities. In order to regain confidence and identity, men need to become more aware of what it truly means to be a Christian man. In other words, they must become Christlike.

Give an example from the life of Jesus when He demonstrated:

physical strength _____

boldness _____

anger _____

rebuke _____

If you need some help, check out these Scriptures: Matthew 12:38-39; 15:7-9; 17:17; 21:12; John 19:8-11.

A Christian father is to raise his sons to understand masculinity without creating insensitive tyrants. Our model is Jesus. He knows how to be gentle as well as firm, merciful and just, bold, yet humble. He was a masculine man. He was a perfect man. Once you begin to have a proper view of Christian masculinity, you can know how to raise masculine sons. Ask God to give you the courage to be a masculine Christian man.

Write a prayer expressing to God your thoughts and feelings about being a Christlike man.

_____

_____

_____

_____

_____

DAY 3
A Father and His Son (Part 2)

Read Ephesians 6:4.

Now that we have discussed what it means to be a masculine man, we can now begin to look at how to raise masculine sons. First we must understand how boys become feminized. On one hand, boys are feminized because many children are raised primarily by women. Divorce, abandonment, and neglect all play a part in America's problem of disappearing fathers. As a result, boys in particular never gain a proper understanding of what it means to be a man. The mother is the only person around to provide information about identity. The result is often a feminized boy.

On the other hand, the father's presence is no guarantee that his sons will be given the proper example and instruction to reach their full potential. Fathers may try too hard to mold perfect children and only cause them to become bitter. This is the other extreme.

Ephesians 6:4 says, "Fathers, do not exasperate your children; instead bring them up in the training and instruction of the Lord." Many kids today are angry and bitter. Our culture is violent. It takes fathers who are willing to be both strong and gentle to lead their kids to the truth.

Do you provoke your children to anger? Write an account of the last time one of your children became angry with you:

_____

_____

_____

Was his or her anger justified? ❑ Yes ❑ No

Was your response justified? ❑ Yes ❑ No

A child's anger does not necessarily mean that you as the father acted or spoke inappropriately. It may simply indicate immaturity, disappointment, or defiance on the part of your child. However, a child's anger should at least provide a warning signal or pause for reflection. Proper discipline should lead a child to repentance, not anger.

William Hendrickson suggests there are at least six ways a father can embitter his children:

1. *By overprotection.* This is one of the most effective ways of feminizing a boy. When you instill within a boy the fear of getting hurt, you are damaging a natural tendency toward bravery and self-sufficiency. Instead of protecting them from getting hurt, a father should be teaching his children good judgment. Children who have been overprotected tend to resent their parents for not giving them necessary courage and wisdom for life.
2. *By favoritism.* When a child realizes that a parent has a favorite, that child will become embittered toward both the parent and the sibling. A father should strive to praise the attributes of all his children and to avoid favoritism.
3. *By discouragement.* Fathers have a great responsibility to use their words wisely. A father can embitter a child permanently simply by saying a few discouraging words. Your children will believe what you say. Discouragement instills within the child a feeling of worthlessness and despair.
4. *By not recognizing a child's independence.* Fathers who want a clone of themselves only succeed in creating the exact opposite most of the time. You need to be aware of and allow for the differences between you and your child. They will only resent being forced into a mold that doesn't fit.
5. *By neglect.* Neglect happens in families on many levels. A father can provide every possible material need to a child, and yet that child may suffer from emotional neglect. Children need parents more than they need things from their parents. A neglected child will suffer insecurity and fear unless the parents step in and provide for the child's true needs.
6. *By violence.* Abusing a child is one of the most devastating ways of embittering a child. Too often, a father will take out his frustration on his children. Abusive behavior includes verbal as well as physical abuse. It is passed from one generation to the next generation. Violence against a child must not happen. A father needs to always maintain control.

Label each of these situations with the number of the method above that the father displays:
____ 1. The father signed his son up for T-ball without asking him.
____ 2. The father told his youngest son how well the older son was doing in math. "Why can't you get it?" he asked. "John is just smarter than you."
____ 3. The father rushed out the door to work. "I'll catch your next concert," he yelled over his shoulder.
____ 4. "I can't believe I produced a lazy slob like you. Go clean up your room," the father snarled.
____ 5. "Let me do that for you," the father said as he took his son's hunting knife.
____ 6. "Why bother?" asked the father "You didn't make the team last year and the same coach is picking."

Have you embittered your child by any of these methods? (check one or more)
❑ overprotection   ❑ favoritism
❑ discouragement   ❑ not recognizing a child's independence
❑ neglect   ❑ violence

"Fathers, do not exasperate your children; instead, bring them up in the training and instruction of the Lord" (Eph. 6:4). As a Christian father, it is your role to raise Christian children. If you are serious about giving your children a proper identity, you will instruct them in the ways of the Lord. Avoid embittering them. Give them a godly example of Christianity.

Ask God for forgiveness for ways you may have exasperated your children. Pray for guidance in raising your children.

DAY 4
A Father and His Daughter

Read Ephesians 5:22-30.

Within Scripture, you won't find many instructions about raising daughters. However, some fundamental guidelines about daughters can be gleaned from Ephesians 5. The basic instructions concerning a husband-and-wife relationship can also teach principles that apply to a father-and-daughter relationship.

In the same way that a husband honors his wife, he should also honor his daughter. By substituting the word *daughter* for *wife*, we can understand how a father is to treat his daughter.

A Father is to Lead His Daughter

Ephesians 5: 23 says, "The husband is the head of the [daughter]." It is your duty to lead your daughter into the knowledge of the truth. She will look to you to be that leader.

As her father, you should:
- Prepare her for godliness, more than being a success.
- Teach her to be respected, more than popular.
- Lead her in righteousness, more than peer approval.
- Praise her for her character, rather than for her appearance.

A Father is to Love His Daughter

Ephesians 5:25 says, "Husbands, love your [daughters], just as Christ loved the church and gave himself up for her." This is a sacrificial love. Your daughter needs to know that you will protect her from harm. Her security will be based on the love she receives from you.

How do you show your daughter your love for her? (circle one or more)

hugs   time spent with her   interest in her friends   kisses

compliments   interest in her activities   praying with her

A Father is to Understand His Daughter

We can apply 1 Peter 3:7 (NASB) here as well. "Live with your [daughters] in an understanding way." Kids are growing up faster these days. They adopt adult attitudes and habits much earlier than we may expect or want them to. As a result, it is difficult to understand what your daughter may be going through. As you try to be understanding toward your wife, you should also be understanding toward your daughter.

To live in a sensitive and understanding way does not mean that you will understand everything about your daughter. It means that you will make every effort to be caring, loving, and concerned.

What is your typical response when your daughter is tearful, moody, or sad? _____

_____

How can you show more understanding? _____

_____

A Father is to Honor His Daughter

As you honor your wife, you should honor your daughter. Daughters need emotional support that they can only receive from their fathers. For each of the following duties of a father, give an example. A father should:

- Edify (teach) her

_____

- Encourage her

_____

- Praise her

_____

Our culture has tough expectations of women. As your daughter grows, she will need your encouragement and support to strengthen her own self-image.

Above all, fathers should give their daughters the hope of Christianity. Only in Christ will they will find fulfillment. They will use your example as a template for their own lives. They will look for a man who resembles you. Be certain you are providing the right example.

Finish the following prayer:
"Lord, help me to provide the right direction for my daughter by _____

_____."

DAY 5
The Role of the Father and Mother

Read 1 Corinthians 11:11-12.

In the passage for today, Paul reminded us that men and women are interdependent—not independent from each other. God created two sexes with distinct purposes and roles. When we live by God's design, men and women complement each other and enhance each other.

Many people today hesitate to say that God has given us specific roles for both genders. To have a biblical family, we must realize that God has given fathers and mothers specific duties and the abilities to carry them out.

Many people have their own opinion about this topic. What do you feel are the specific roles for fathers and mothers in a biblical family?

A father's role is _____

_____.

A mother's role is _____

_____.

Within the family, two needs must be met—provision and care. A family must be provided and cared for. This naturally leads to two distinct roles within the family unit.

Who is the main provider in your family? _____

Who is the main caregiver in your family? _____

Today there are fewer and fewer models of traditional families. In our society, many people have chosen to maintain two incomes for provision. Often, the result is a family in which the children are raised primarily by someone other than the parents. Children raised in this type of environment learn that it is a normal and proper way to live.

Even though our culture has invented many types of care-giving facilities to take the place of the family, God has an ideal plan for the family. From the beginning, God intended that families have both parents actively involved in childrearing.

The Christian model maintains that the husband is the head of the home. This does not mean that he is the dictator, but that he is the one whom God will hold responsible for the family. Out of love and respect for his wife and children, he will lead them. The wife's role is to help guide the family through love and care. She is the partner from whom the husband will seek advice and support.

This relationship is modeled best by Christ and the church. The church is the bride of Christ, loving and honoring Him. Christ, in turn, is the head of the church, laying down His life for His bride.

Christ leads through humility and sacrificial love. If a husband will lead his wife in the same way, she is more able and willing to honor and respect him. The worldly man does not lead in this way. He finds this model old-fashioned and offensive. We must remember that our obligation is to God as we aim to raise godly families.

Although the father is the primary provider and the mother is the primary caregiver, these role assignments should not give the father license to become a workaholic and leave the rearing of children to his wife. Check the following ways you can care for your children as a means of bonding with them, establishing good communication, and modeling Christlike behavior:

- ❏ feeding infants
- ❏ bathing younger children
- ❏ changing diapers
- ❏ carpooling children to activities
- ❏ reading to your child
- ❏ other _____

- ❏ working with the children in the yard
- ❏ working with the children on household tasks
- ❏ helping with homework
- ❏ going on school field trips

Place an X on the scale to answer the question: How am I balancing provision and care?

all provision, no care   provision, some care   provision plus care   all care, little provision

Obviously, if fathers are to be involved in the lives of their children, they are going to have to be willing to say no to some opportunities—and even work demands—that would effectively take them out of the picture at home. In which of the following ways would you be willing to sacrifice to spend time with your family? (check)

- ❏ turn down a traveling job
- ❏ turn down a promotion
- ❏ turn down overtime
- ❏ take time away from work during the day

- ❏ reduce amount of work brought home
- ❏ avoid being on call 24-7
- ❏ limit computer/television time until children are in bed
- ❏ value family togetherness above material "stuff"

Pray the following prayer as you strive to fulfill your role.

"Lord, help me to be the husband that You desire me to be. Give me the strength and courage to lead my family in humility and love sacrificially just as You love."

WEEK 6

UNDERSTANDING
THE TIMES

VIEWER GUIDE

Leadership can be classified as either _____ or _____.

Saul didn't have a heart for _____. He didn't have a heart _____ _____.

David was a man after God's own _____. He had the heart for _____.

Whenever a synthetic leader meets an authentic leader …

- The synthetic leader gets _____ and _____.

- Synthetic leaders have to _____ the authentic leader.

If we can't understand our _____, how can we effectively lead?

Three observations about our times:

1. The _____ are being destroyed.

2. _____ is no longer essential.

3. We are _____ for judgment.

We allow the world to _____ _____ rather than _____ _____ the world.

DAY 1
Authentic Leadership

Read 1 Samuel 13:13-14.

I have defined a leader as someone who leads. Leadership does not mean a position of leadership. Not everyone in a position of leadership is an effective leader. Today we are going to discuss the differences between authentic and synthetic leaders.
- Authentic leaders lead out of the character and motivation that makes up their lives.
- Synthetic leaders resemble authentic leaders but lack the true motivations of leadership.

Genuine leadership always threatens synthetic leaders. Synthetic leaders are intimidated by real leaders. Authentic leaders never need a title; they lead out of the power of their lives.

Our society is full of leaders of both types. Below list six persons who are portrayed in the media as leaders. Beside each name you list, put an A if you consider that person an authentic leader or an S if you consider that person a synthetic leader.

_____   _____

_____   _____

_____   _____

In Scripture, we can find a poignant example of synthetic leadership in King Saul. Being king, Saul had the perfect leadership title. He even looked like a leader. The problem was that he had no interior convictions to support his title. His failure was a failure of the heart. Saul repeatedly sought to kill David because King Saul felt threatened by the young man.

In contrast to Saul, we find an authentic leader in Israel's next king—David. When David first met Saul, he was full of faith and conviction. Saul immediately recognized his character. David's authenticity was proved in 1 Samuel, which calls David "a man after his (God's) own heart" (13:14).

Many of David's men saw David's ability and supported him in his struggle. These men were referred to as the "mighty men" of David. According to 1 Chronicles 12:32, the Sons of Issachar had a special insight. These men "understood the times and knew what Israel should do." Men like the Sons of Issachar were important because David needed leaders who could lead out of knowledge and wisdom.

Our homes and our nation are in a leadership crisis today. As a nation, we must begin to find leaders with moral conviction and heart. We need leaders who lead in the right direction. We need leaders like the Sons of Issachar who understand the times we live in and are effective in their leadership decisions. A man who understands his times possesses the characteristics of vision and discernment.

Why do you think vision and discernment are important? Finish the following statements:

A leader must have vision because _____

_____

A leader must be discerning because _____

_____

Vision allows a leader to understand what is happening now and will probably happen in the future. A leader must be able to anticipate events in order to prepare for them. Once a leader has vision, he must be discerning in order to make wise decisions. Discernment guides a leader to take appropriate actions.

Very briefly stated, what is your vision for your family?

_____

_____

This week, we will try to understand our times. As the leader of your home, you need to be aware of what the world really believes. You need to have a vision for where your family is going. You must learn discernment in order to lead your family down the narrow path of truth. Your leadership will be effective only if you acquire these skills.

Write a prayer, asking God to give you eyes that see and ears that hear. Your family's moral excellence depends on your leadership. Pray that God will enable you to be an authentic leader.

_____

_____

_____

_____

DAY 2
Moral Foundations

Read Psalm 11:3.

We live in the midst of a gigantic struggle between two opposing life systems. In *How Now Shall We Live?* Chuck Colson identifies these two life systems as the biblical and naturalist worldviews.[1] Our nation was founded on a biblical worldview. The foundational beliefs that make up a biblical worldview include that:

- God is the creator of our universe.
- Personal sin is to blame for what has gone wrong in our world.
- The solution is to be found in and through God's truth and laws.

The biblical worldview has been largely replaced in modern society by the naturalist worldview that allows no place for right or wrong. The modern attitude makes personal choice the only absolute to be observed.

If we are going to influence our world today, we must become aware of the change that has taken place. The United States had a specific foundation. The founding fathers' single most important influence was the Bible. Judeo-Christian morality served as the basis for our laws, our constitution, and our freedom. We cannot say that all the founding fathers were believers, but we do know the foundations they laid were based on biblical principles.

One of the most basic principles that underlies out country is the existence of moral absolutes. Today many people have been taught that there are no moral absolutes. How do you define a moral absolute?

A moral absolute is _____

_____.

We know from nature that certain universal laws cannot be broken. We call these absolutes.

- Gravity is an absolute.
- The earth's rotation around the sun is an absolute.
- Death is an absolute.

Certain moral absolutes also exist.

- Human life is sacred.
- Actions such as lying, cheating, and adultery are sins against a Holy God.
- We are accountable to God for our attitudes and actions.

Right and wrong are ultimately based on the character of God. Because our secular world says God does not exist, it also insists that moral absolutes do not exist. Secularists believe that everything is relative and that truth is subjective. They teach that One True God is the figment of your imagination, but lesser gods of your own creation are acceptable.

Without God as the foundation, our society has nothing on which to stand. Psalm 11:3 says, "When the foundations are being destroyed, what can the righteous do?" The righteous can take a stand and lead their families and communities into the truth. The righteous can remain faithful to God and His precepts.

What foundations in our country are being destroyed? (check those that apply)
❑ God   ❑ truth
❑ sanctity of life   ❑ freedom

How can you equip yourself and your family to confront the challenges in each area you identified as being under attack?

God _____

Truth _____

Sanctity of Life _____

Freedom _____

During the time known as the Dark Ages, barbarians threatened civilization. However, certain groups of Christians preserved the faith in small communities. Within these communities:
• God's Word was read and obeyed.
• Women were respected.
• Leaders were developed.
• Morality was practiced.
• Discipline was expected.
• Accountability was the order of the day (*Standing Tall*, 222-223).

These same factors must characterize our families today. To preserve our foundations, we must raise children in the Word of God. We must pass on belief in the moral absolutes and practice the virtues of Jesus. The world may be against us, but the Lord is with us.

Write a brief prayer, asking the Lord to help you and your family stand tall on His foundations.

_____

_____

_____

DAY 3
Standing for Truth

Read John 8:31-32.

Because our country's foundations are being destroyed, much of the moral fiber of this nation is being compromised. Morality was once viewed as either black and white. Today morality is gray. The absolutes we once believed in are now relative. Truth is no longer essential but has become optional.

Known as moral relativism, this philosophy claims that God does not exist. By eliminating God, moral relativism eliminates the moral absolutes that are a part of Him. With no moral absolutes, people are free to determine their own brand of morality or immorality.

Believing in the concept of moral absolutes does not guarantee that we always act out of our beliefs. From your Bible read Exodus 20:1-17. Place a check below by the commandments you have broken.
- ❏ (v. 3) substituting church attendance for giving God priority in your life
- ❏ (v. 4) making an idol of work, a possession, or a hobby
- ❏ (v. 7) using curse words; using God's name in a casual or disrespectful way
- ❏ (v. 8) using the Lord's day as a work day
- ❏ (v. 12) failing to call or contact your parent(s) on special occasions; forgetting special events in their lives
- ❏ (vs. 13-17) violating the spirit if not the letter of these laws

The laws that govern our nation were based on absolute truth, God's truth. When the truth is questioned, the laws that stand on it become undermined.
- You cannot have a nation without truth.
- You cannot have a family without truth.
- You cannot have a healthy relationship without truth.

Jesus said, " 'If you hold to my teaching, you are really my disciples. Then you will know the truth, and the truth will set you free' " (John 8:31-32). God's Word is truth. Without it, nothing will have meaning.

If any more evidence is necessary to prove that America has changed, William Bennett, the former Secretary of Education, provides it in his *Index of Leading Cultural Indicators*. The results are astonishing and demonstrate just how great the changes in this country have been since the early 1960s.
- An increase in violent crime of 560 percent.
- More than a 400-percent increase in illegitimate births.

- Quadrupling of divorce rates.
- Tripling of the percentage of children living in single-parent homes.
- More than a 200-percent increase in teenage suicide.
- A drop of almost 80 points in the S.A.T. scores (*Standing Tall,* 21).

When the foundations are shaken and the truth is questioned, a nation turns to evil. Our nation is in great peril. We need men who will stand for the truth. We need fathers who will give their children a legacy of faith, hope, love, and truth.

As our world becomes increasingly immoral, we need to equip our children with God's Word so they will know what is true and good. Ask yourself a few important questions:
- How can I teach my children the truth in tangible ways?
- Do I take every opportunity to present the truth to those around me by the words I say and the way I live?

Take a few moments to think of ways you can stand up for the truth in the following areas:

At work, I can stand for the truth by _____

_____.

At home, I can stand for the truth by _____

_____.

In my marriage, I can stand for the truth by _____

_____.

With my children, I can stand for the truth by _____

_____.

As a Christian, you are a bastion of the truth in a perilous world. As you stand for what is right and what is good, you are preaching the gospel of Christ. By living the truth, you are setting yourself free, and you are leading others to freedom by your example. Stand firm in the truth.

Finish the following prayer, asking the Lord to empower you to boldly live the truth every day.

"Lord, I thank You for the freedom You have granted me in Your truth. Now help me live the truth by

_____

_____."

DAY 4
The Need for Repentance

Read Romans 1:18-20.

As our country turns away from God, moral absolutes, and the truth, we begin to reap the judgment of God. This judgment does not necessarily mean fire and brimstone; it may come in many different forms. God may simply give our nation over to the sin and debauchery we desire. We sentence ourselves to death by turning away from the One who is life.

Arnold Toynby looked at 20 of the great civilizations in the history of the world. Each of those civilizations rose to greatness and then collapsed. Toynby discovered each civilization went through five stages:
- initial beginnings
- growth and expansion
- preservation of gains made
- moral degeneracy
- collapse

In your opinion, what stage is America in today? _____

Our country has seen the first three stages, and we are living in the frightening reality of the fourth. God has blessed this nation from the beginning, and we have turned our backs on Him. We are choosing our own self-gratification and lusts over the Lord. Our nation is in trouble.

How would you describe the moral degeneracy that our country now embraces? Write several biblically immoral practices that have become common in our country.

1. _____

2. _____

3. _____

Today's morality is anything but biblical. God has promised that the road that leads to destruction is wide. Our nation is on that wide road. You must decide if you and your family are going to stay on that road or if you are going to choose the narrow path that leads to eternal life.

Our country promotes tolerance for all ways of life. The result is that we live in a country in which every type of immoral lifestyle is welcomed and encouraged. Your children will be the heirs of a nation of idolaters.

If we look at the Old Testament, we can see God's judgment coming severely on the people who disobeyed Him. His judgment was devastating against Syria, Babylon, Israel, and Judah.

In more modern times, we have seen the collapse of the Soviet Union. Was that God's judgment? The Soviets promoted atheism, humanism, terror, and hate. Any nation that practices such characteristics will never be blessed by God. God allowed these nations to fall. If the United States continues its fall into moral debauchery, God will allow us to suffer as well.

What do you think God's judgment will be like? _____

_____

Finish this sentence: If the United States continues on its path of moral degeneracy, _____

_____.

A nation that expels God from its life invites death and destruction. We cannot expect God to continue to protect us from ourselves. Romans 1:24-25 says, "Therefore God gave them over in the sinful desires of their hearts to sexual impurity for the degrading of their bodies with one another. They exchanged the truth of God for a lie, and worshiped and served created things rather than the Creator."

In reality, our country fits that description. God will hand us over to our sinful desires if we continue to ignore and hate Him. We need to live faithful and repentant lives. As a nation, we need to repent and stand for God, absolute truth, morality, faith, and belief.

Let us prepare for what may come. Live a life of truth. Teach your children what is good and right. Share with others the good news of Christ that God may save us. Write a brief prayer for our country. Begin by repenting of your own sins. Then ask the Lord to bring our country to repentance.

_____

_____

_____

_____

_____

DAY 5
Important Questions

Read Ephesians 5:8-16.

Understanding our times requires a person to look at our world with vision and discernment, not to long for times gone by. As leaders, we must make every effort to understand what forces and philosophies are shaping our world. We can no longer afford to wait. If our nation is to be saved, now is the time.

To begin our efforts, we need to ask a few questions:

What Kind of Leader Are You?

Is your leadership more authentic or synthetic? As a leader, your vision for the future must be accompanied by discernment. Do you strive to understand the times, or are you stuck in ignorance about the modern world? Do you study and prepare yourself to confront the ideas that challenge your family?
- ❑ I actively seek to prepare myself and my family.
- ❑ I just try to do the best I can.
- ❑ other _____

Paul wrote Timothy telling him to: "Do your best to present yourself to God as one approved, a workman who does not need to be ashamed and who correctly handles the word of truth" (2 Tim. 2:15) Similarly, Peter told us all to "Always be prepared to give an answer to everyone who asks you to give the reason for the hope that you have" (1 Pet. 3:15). Certainly that preparedness needs to begin at home and with our children.

How Are You Rebuilding the Foundations?

Your first priority is to give your family a solid foundation. We can no longer expect society to uphold any morality or traditions for us. It is the father's duty to instill within his children a sense of purpose and value. To accomplish this, a father must think practically. You cannot drive a moral education into your children. You must be able to think creatively of ways to give your children values without making them resent you.

At the top of the next page you will find some simple suggestions of ways to show your children the foundations you possess and the wisdom you would like to pass on. Check the suggestions you already practice. Put an X by the ones you'd like to implement with your family. Write other ways you would like to try to pass on these foundations and wisdom.

❑ Read the Bible every day.
❑ Spend time together regularly and often.
❑ Let your children see you honor and respect your wife.

❑ Pray together every day.
❑ Attend church regularly.
❑ Take your children with you when you are able.

❑ _____

Foundations for life are built slowly. Every day is an opportunity to strengthen those foundations. If they are strong, the lives your children build will be a testament to the faithfulness of God and the work of His servant.

Are You Living Out the Truth?

In our society, truth is difficult to find. We face many situations daily where the truth can be stretched or completely overlooked. As a Christian, you have the opportunity to practice the truth wherever you are. Total devotion to the truth will enable you to live the truth daily. Ephesians 5:8-10 says, "For you were once darkness, but now you are light in the Lord. Live as children of light (for the fruit of the light consists in all goodness, righteousness and truth) and find out what pleases the Lord." Our calling is to be the children of light in everything we do.

In what situations is it easier not to tell the truth?

1. _____

2. _____

Why is telling the truth in these situations so difficult? _____

_____

Will you commit to being a man of truth and living the truth in every situation? (circle) Yes No

Are You Prepared for God's Judgment?

People in our world live in ignorance. They believe the philosophy "eat, drink, and be merry for tomorrow we die." They foresee no consequences for their sinful behavior. The truth remains. Every day is an opportunity for repentance—don't waste it on anything else. God has given us His Word and His Spirit to lead us. Be certain you are living to please Him.

Write a brief prayer, asking for God's help to live this life of truth. It is only by His hand that we can find peace and joy.

_____

_____

_____

WEEK 7

A ONE-WOMAN KIND OF MAN

VIEWER GUIDE

In the Christian life, some assembly is _____.

We have been given

- the Word of God

- the Spirit of God

- the church of God.

Keeping faith is a reference to the _____ of God.

Keep a nerve of conscience that is _____ to the Holy Spirit of God.

The primary area the enemy is going to try to bring us down in is the _____ area.

Five ways to be a one-woman kind of man:

1. With my _____

2. With my _____

3. With my _____

4. With my _____

5. With my _____

DAY 1
Fight the Good Fight

Read 1 Timothy 1:18-19.

The Christian life is a struggle, a journey that contains many ups and downs along the way. But preparation has been made for us. Peter said that God has given us everything we need pertaining to life and godliness.
- He has given us the Word of God.
- He has given us the Spirit of God.
- He has given us the church.

God has given us every tool that is required to survive in this world. However, Philippians 2:12-13 says, "Work out your salvation with fear and trembling, for it is God who works in you to will and to act according to his good purpose." It is the Lord Himself who is at work within us, transforming us into His image. Our responsibility is to work with Him.

In your lifetime, you will probably face many difficulties and confrontations. Temptation to sin lies around every corner and the enemy is trying to make you stumble whenever he can.

For men, one of the most difficult temptations comes in the area of sexuality. Men are sexual creatures made with sexual drives and feelings. As a Christian man, your duty is to decide what to do with those drives. You can either let them control you and degrade your body, or you can work to harness them and allow God to direct them into purity and holiness.

Do you know someone who has fallen into sexual impurity? _____

How did it affect his life and family? _____

_____

Purity and holiness are acquired through the fruit of the spirit known as self-control. Self-control is a battle that you face in many ways every day of your life. The enemy knows your weaknesses and will stop at nothing to bring you down.

In 1 Timothy 1:18 we have a letter of encouragement from Paul to Timothy. Due to his youth and inexperience, Timothy had become discouraged. To build him up, Paul wrote, "I give you this instruction in keeping with the prophecies once made about you, so that by following them you may fight the good fight."

What is the *good fight* Paul spoke about? _____

If you are uncertain what you are fighting for, you will have little success. The *good fight* is the Christian life. It is a struggle between our old nature and the new nature that we received when we accepted Jesus Christ. Our old nature leads to death, but the Lord offers peace and joy for eternity. That is why we must wage war against the old self.

Paul continued by saying, "that by following them you may fight the good fight, holding on to faith and a good conscience. Some have rejected these and so have shipwrecked their faith" (v. 18-19).

How do we fight the good fight? By holding on to faith. By having a good conscience.

Name several ways that you hold on to the Christian faith:

_____

_____.

You can only have faith if you know what to have faith in. To have faith in God, you must read and understand His Word. You must know Him in an intimate way. You must let Him lead, even when you don't know on the front end how everything will turn out. Faith requires putting feet to your prayers by stepping out into the unknown with Him.

The *good fight* is not contained by faith alone. The second part of this fight is to keep a good conscience. David said, "I have hidden your word in my heart that I might not sin against you" (Ps. 119:11). This is how to keep a good conscience.

How is a *good conscience* formed?

_____.

How often do you listen to your conscience?

            Never   Rarely   Sometimes   Often   All the time

Your conscience is the internal nerve that allows you to know right from wrong. The conscience is that part of us God uses to lead us to repentance. However, we can kill our own conscience by numbing it with sin. We can dull its ability to feel and harden our hearts.

God wants you to keep the faith. He wants you to practice the faith by keeping a good conscience. These two are meant to work together. This week we will be looking at specific ways of keeping a good conscience. With God's help, we can fight the good fight and be men worthy of our calling.

Pray: *"Lord, help me to maintain a good conscience by putting godly virtues into action. Soften my heart so that I can hear Your voice. Grant me the humility I need to be a Christian man and give me strength in this struggle. Amen."*

DAY 2
Develop Good Character

Read 1 Timothy 3:1-5.

In day 1 Paul reminded us that keeping the faith and having a good conscience are vital to the Christian life, which he described as *the good fight.* Christian men everywhere are in a war. The enemy can easily blindside us. A man who does not practice self-control on a daily basis will be an easy target. Then individual sins become a sinful lifestyle. Once a pattern of sin has settled in, it becomes a comfort zone.

- You rationalize the sins you are committing.
- You convince yourself it is not all that bad.
- You convince yourself everyone is doing it.

Paul wrote his letter to Timothy, a fellow minister. You may ask, *Why is this teaching important if I'm not in the ministry?* The fact is, if you are a Christian, you are in the ministry. If you are a husband, you are in the ministry. You are in the ministry of Christian leadership. Leadership to one degree or another is the calling of every man. Therefore, all men should seek the qualities of a good leader.

In 1 Timothy 3:1-2 we read, "If anyone sets his heart on being an overseer, he desires a noble task. Now the overseer must be above reproach, the husband of but one wife." These first two qualities are the backbone of a godly man.

What does to be above reproach mean to you? _____

_____

To be above reproach has everything to do with character and reputation. You need to be so vigorous and dedicated to your practice of godliness that no one can ever say anything wrong about you. People should know that you strive diligently to glorify God by your lifestyle.

We have many examples of leaders who are not above reproach. They are cunning and deceitful and try to avoid the light of truth as much as possible. You should avoid their example; be above reproach in everything you do.

Can you think of an area of your life where you are not above reproach? Pause right now and ask God to forgive you and cleanse this area of your life. Thank Him for His forgiveness. Commit this area to Him.

The second part of the verse reads, "the husband of but one wife." The verse literally says a "one-woman man." Many people interpret this verse to simply mean you cannot be divorced. The truth is, a man can be married to one woman and still be unfaithful in his mind, emotions, and body. This week we are reminding ourselves to be a one-woman kind of man.

How can a man be a one-woman man ...

• mentally? _____

_____

• emotionally? _____

_____

• physically? _____

_____

Purity is a virtue that should be practiced by Christian men every day of their lives. To be the husband of one wife requires a man to be dedicated to her mentally, emotionally, and physically. A godly man understands this single-minded devotion. A godly man practices purity every day of his life.

Probably the most effective and destructive attack the enemy can use is in the area of sexual temptation. Proverbs 7:21-23 describes it this way:

"With persuasive words, she led him astray;
    she seduced him with her smooth talk.
All at once he followed her
    like an ox going to the slaughter,
like a deer stepping into a noose,
    till an arrow pierces his liver,
like a bird darting into a snare,
    little knowing it will cost him his life."

The rest of this week we will be looking at specific and practical ways to be "a one-woman kind of man." Satan is subtle in his attacks, and we can be equally as clever in our justification for sin. Be open to conviction, and allow God to make you pure in heart and body.

Take time to pray, asking God to help you to be above reproach and to be a one-woman kind of man.

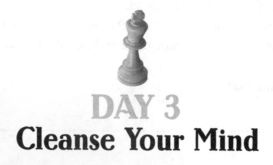

DAY 3
Cleanse Your Mind

Read Romans 12:1-2.

The human mind is a private place. No person can enter your thought-life. God alone knows what secrets you keep there. The mind is the entry point in spiritual warfare. The enemy seeks to influence our minds in order to influence our behavior. Paul wrote in Romans 12:2, "Do not conform any longer to the pattern of this world, but be transformed by the renewing of your mind."

When it comes to sexuality, what is the pattern of this world?
- ❑ If it feels good, do it.
- ❑ Lust is natural.
- ❑ Fantasizing is acceptable.
- ❑ I can't help it.

Paul said that we must be transformed by our mind's renewal. All kinds of sophisticated philosophies exist. A man who wants to lead his family must learn to sift through the wrong ideas and take them captive to the obedience of Christ.

Bill Hull writes that a man "must know the Bible well enough, through study, to fight temptation and protect himself against the ideas and philosophies of the world. [He] is confronted daily with thousands of messages and ideas. A biblical defense system must sort out the ideas, take what is obedient to Christ, and reject what is not" (*Point Man,* 98).

Let's look at this realistically:
- You cannot entirely prevent wrong thoughts from coming into your mind.
- You can decide what to do with those thoughts.
- A consistent pattern of rejecting ungodly thoughts will make them less likely to occur. Indulging the thoughts will most likely encourage them to recur.

Temptation is that moment when a thought occurs. Sin is allowing temptation to grow into a pattern of thought that will eventually lead to action. The man who is grounded in the Word of God will be able to resist that temptation through the power of the Holy Spirit.

From the following list, check where you most often encounter temptation:
- ❑ at work
- ❑ in front of the television
- ❑ out with friends
- ❑ in magazines
- ❑ in the car
- ❑ on the Internet
- ❑ when I am alone
- ❑ at sports events

The fact is, you are going to encounter temptation in our sex-saturated society. This statement is not license to indulge the sinful nature by exposing yourself to sexual temptation. James said to resist temptation (Jas. 4:7).

In the Old Testament, the Jews were given specific laws that dealt primarily with external sin. They were laws such as: do not commit murder, do not commit adultery, and do not bear false witness against your neighbor.

When Christ came, He fulfilled that law by giving us the meaning behind it. In addition to the laws fighting sin externally, Christ provides ways of fighting sin in the heart. Christ said: do not hate, do not lust, and do not have a heart of deceit.

Most of us are pretty capable of keeping the external law, but we continue to struggle with the internal where sin is born and bred. We should strive to take every thought captive for Christ. Sin's battle is lost or won in our thoughts.

What is the problem with impure thoughts? _____

_____

Recall that our week is titled "A One-Woman Kind of Man." Can we truly say we are a one-woman man if we are only faithful with our physical bodies? What effects does sexual fantasizing have on the marriage relationship? What effects does it have on our pursuit of godliness? Check one or more problems with impure thoughts.

❑ Causes dissatisfaction with our marriage partner.

❑ Discourages us in our spiritual walk.

❑ Leads to guilt and shame.

❑ Requires greater and greater stimulation to produce the same effect.

❑ Sets us up for emotional entanglements with another woman.

❑ Ultimately results in physical unfaithfulness.

Christ would have you flee immorality. Do not entertain lustful desires in your heart. They always lead to more grievous sins. Don't be discouraged if this sounds difficult. God will strengthen you to do the good work. The Holy Spirit will soften your heart to His pleading. The Lord will guide you as you choose the paths of righteousness. Allow God to take every thought captive. Cleanse your mind.

"Lord, you know the darkness of my heart and the weakness of my spirit. Help me to be pure. Create in me a clean heart and renew a right spirit within me. It is for You my soul longs. Give me the strength to carry on. Amen."

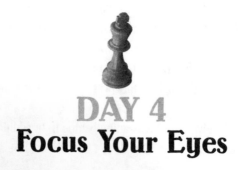

DAY 4
Focus Your Eyes

Read Job 31:1.

A one-woman kind of man demonstrates his commitment by disciplining his eyes. Our eyes are the windows into our minds. What we see is forever burned into our memories. The enemy knows this, and he will offer you endless opportunities to fall to temptation through your eyes.

What specific types of actions do you think Job did to carry out the commitment he made in Job 31:1?

_____

_____

Within your mind, you have the capability of changing many sights into sin. The difficulty is that we may see things we often did not want or intend to see. Just living each day puts us into situations in which we will look at something or someone and be tempted to sin.

It is impossible not to notice a beautiful woman or a seductive picture, but because of your commitment to be a one-woman kind of man with your eyes, you don't look at women in a way that would diminish your commitment to God and to your wife. A godly man cultivates a special kind of *blindness*.

Job said, "I made a covenant with my eyes not to look lustfully at a girl" (1:1). Notice here he desired not to look at the girl lustfully. He was specific in his intention. He knew that to be lustful would diminish his character and commitment.

Lust is harmful for many reasons. Why do you think God's Word so consistently warns us about lust?

_____

_____

Lust degrades you and the object of your lust. When you commit lust in your heart, you are serving the corrupt, sinful nature from which Christ died to free you. Lust requires looking at women as objects, not as persons for whom Christ died. Lust is a cruel master; it makes you a slave to your passions and desires. Lust is a killer of healthy relationships with the opposite sex. It undermines your relationship with your wife.

How do you become chaste with your eyes? It requires a pre-determined plan of action.
- Know how you are going to deal with temptation before you ever encounter it.
- Decide how you are going to treat the things you see.
- Anticipate how you will react to a situation.

Describe how you are going to deal with temptation in the following situations:
1. Your wife subscribes to a magazine that usually contains advertisements of lingerie and other sexually-stimulating clothing. She leaves it lying on the bedside table.
2. A coworker is known for having inappropriate pictures tacked to his cubicle walls.
3. A seductive picture is plastered on a billboard that is on your route home from work.
4. Your son wants to put a pin-up on his wall at home.

Because you never know when temptation will occur, it is vital to plan ahead what you will do. If you find that you are tempted when you are on the Internet, make a plan never to use it while you are alone. If temptation strikes while you are watching television, use the remote control or turn it off. If certain magazines or newspapers contain sexually stimulating material, avoid them like a plague. The struggle for purity must be proactive. It is a struggle you can't afford to lose.

In Matthew 5, Jesus described a radical way of avoiding sin: "If your right eye causes you to sin, gouge it out and throw it away. It is better for you to lose one part of your body than for your whole body to be thrown into hell. And if your right hand causes you to sin, cut it off and throw it away. It is better for you to lose one part of your body than for your whole body to go into hell."

Christ is trying to communicate the degree of seriousness that avoiding sin should have. You must make every effort to maintain purity in your life.

What can Christian men do to mobilize our society to reduce the amount of sexually-stimulating material that is used in advertising, television programming, on magazine covers, and at sporting events, to name a few?

_____

_____

List one way you can take action where you live:

_____

Write a brief prayer, asking the Lord to help you deal with temptations that you see. Ask that He will give you the strength to maintain purity in your heart and mind.

_____

_____

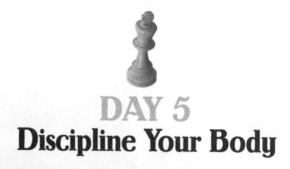

DAY 5
Discipline Your Body

Read 2 Timothy 2:22.

A man must be careful with every part of his being if he is to be a one-woman kind of man. Obviously, we should be careful with our mind and with our eyes, but we must be careful with our whole body if we are to remain pure. Today we are going to look at three more areas that we must maintain—our lips, hands, and feet.

A One-Woman Kind of Man with My Lips

The words that you say with your mouth hold a tremendous amount of power. You have the power to persuade, to injure, and to seduce. It is all too easy for a man to speak without thinking. Often we say things that we probably shouldn't.

You must be careful with the words you say. You must be especially careful with the type of conversations you have with women. A one-woman kind of man is not a flirt. Some men find that their flirtatious behavior comes naturally. That kind of quality can be dangerous for a man who is trying to be dedicated to one woman.

What kind of situations are flirtatious? Below are some examples. List several more that you can think of:
- ❏ Telling a woman she looks particularly nice.
- ❏ Telling a woman a crass joke.
- ❏ Regular phone conversations with a woman other than your wife.

❏ _____

❏ _____

A Christian man must be careful with the words he uses. It is all too easy to fall into inappropriate conversations with other women. Avoid frivolous or crass conversations and protect your commitment to your wife.

A One-Woman Kind of Man with My Hands

To be a one-woman kind of man with your hands, you must be careful with the way you physically touch other women. Within the Christian community, people have a special affection for hugging. This can be done in a healthy and appropriate way, but it can also be done with an entirely different objective in mind.

Are you more physical with certain women than others? ❑ Yes ❑ No

If so, can you explain why? _____

_____

It is important that your conduct with women be appropriate. There should never be any suspicion as to your intentions or actions. If you find yourself hugging women with no particular reason, you might want to examine your motives. It is far better that you maintain distance than become ensnared in sin.

A One-Woman Kind of Man with My Feet

The final way you can preserve your commitment to your wife is by using your feet to flee immorality. You may sometimes find yourself in a compromising situation. What is your first reaction when faced with this situation?

_____

If you are truly committed to being a one-woman kind of man, you will do everything you can to get out of the situation. You will use your feet to run away from the danger. If you are more concerned about your soul than your pride, you will leave as quickly as possible.

What kind of situations might require you to flee immorality? List a situation you have been in that you left or should have left:

_____

_____

_____

_____

Often, for a man to protect his commitment, he must use his feet to get away from a bad situation. Whether at work, at home, or during recreation, the enemy finds clever ways to put temptation before you.

Second Timothy 2:22 says, "Flee the evil desires of youth, and pursue righteousness, faith, love and peace, along with those who call on the Lord out of a pure heart." A believer must take serious action. To be able to flee evil desire, you must pursue God with a pure heart.

Make a commitment to God today to be pure with your words, hands, and feet. The more you practice purity in your heart, the closer you will be to God and the better leader you will be in your home, church, and job. Write a brief prayer, asking the Holy Spirit to help guide you along the path of righteousness and to keep you far from wickedness.

WEEK 8

FINISHING STRONG

VIEWER GUIDE

In the Christian life, it's not so much how you _____ that counts, it's how you _____.

Four Traits of Failure:

1. No _____ _____ in God's Word.

- Plan a _____

- Plan a _____

- Make a _____ _____

- Get in _____ _____

2. No personal _____.

3. Improper _____ with _____.

4. "It will never happen to _____."

If you want to finish strong, here are four *stay's* you should consider.

STAY in the _____.

STAY close to a _____.

STAY away _____ from women you're not married to.

STAY _____.

DAY 1
Live Purposefully

Read Hebrews 12:1.

Have you thought about your future lately? Where do you want to be spiritually in 5, 10, or 20 years?

Chances are, you can only imagine yourself growing spiritually. No one ever believes that they will fall away from the Lord or lose the things in life they now hold dear. But the truth remains: many men will fail to reach the end of their lives living with God.

Most men who start out strong in the faith will fall because of discouragement, sin, or disbelief. The Christian life is a marathon that takes all your strength and stamina. In a marathon, it is not how you start that counts, but how you finish.
- It is the rare man who finishes strong.
- It is the exceptional man who finishes strong.
- It is the teachable man who finishes strong.

"It's endurance that determines whether or not a man will finish strong. And endurance is the fruit of godly character" (*Finishing Strong,* 11). Endurance does not necessarily mean that you will never have weak times. Endurance is the ability to keep on going, to keep the goal in mind even when you feel like giving up.

How many men do you know who were strong in the faith at one time but have now turned aside? _____

Why do you think this happened to them? _____

_____

_____

Many things can happen in life to take a person off the journey. The enemy is subtle and in no hurry. He will wait as long as it takes to sidetrack you. A Christian man can never get comfortable or think that he has arrived. Such men are on the brink of some action or inaction that will result in their failure to finish their race well.

You may be thinking that it is too late for you to finish strong. You have made mistakes such as experiencing a messy divorce, a sexual affair, or serious moral or ethical choices that have caused you to lose credibility.

I want to encourage you to remember that God is greater than any past sin in your life. It is never too late to do what is right. It is never too late to live a life of repentance. The goal is to finish strong, and that requires a man to turn to God daily. Finishing strong begins today.

To finish strong does not mean to finish unblemished or perfect. That is impossible. All men are sinners and all will have dark periods in their lives. Many of the men in Scripture had surprising lives. Many were previously involved in sexual immorality; waited until late in life to submit to God; were considered at mid-life to be utter failures; found themselves stuck in bitter circumstances not of their own making; or overcame personal failure and major setbacks by embracing the grace of God.

Every man's journey is unique. Every man will have situations that the Lord allowed him to bear. A man, through the power of God, must endure these situations. The Lord will give strength and encouragement all along the way. It is through His help that a man can finish the race as a victor.

To finish strong, you need to have a goal in mind. This week we will look at specific reasons why men fall from the faith. When you have a goal in mind and you keep working toward that goal, you will eventually arrive.

What is your purpose? What do you want to do with the rest of your life? Write your "mission statement."

_____

_____

_____

Writing specific goals you want to attain will enable you to achieve your vision for the future. Use the following space to write at least two measurable goals for the immediate future (6 weeks to 6 months):

1. _____

_____

2. _____

_____

If you live every day working toward finishing strong, you will achieve your goals.

Pray the following prayer as you run your race:

"Lord Jesus, the race You have set before me is one that I cannot handle. It is only by Your strength and love that I will be able to endure to the end. Help me in all things to rely upon Your holy name. Be my comforter and guide, for You are great and the only salvation of humankind. Amen."

DAY 2
Stay in the Word

Read Matthew 4:4.

Dr. Howard Hendricks studied 246 men in the ministry who had fallen into sexual immorality within a 24-month period of time. Roughly three ministers a week for two years succumbed to temptation and fell into sin.

Hendricks noted each man demonstrated four common traits prior to his sin. Today we will look at the first of these traits—that these men no longer maintained a personal time in the Word of God. They simply stopped reading the Bible personally.

As pastors, they had to use Scripture to preach and teach, but each failed to spend time in the Word for personal growth. They stopped being private worshippers. Their lives become so busy and confused, they stopped feeding on the only true Source of sustenance.

The ministers shared the same excuses:
- They never intended to stop reading the Word.
- Their lives were so busy with ministry, they were unable to focus personally.
- They felt they would be fine without it.

These men became so busy doing good things, they did not realize they were not doing the best thing. The best thing for men to do is to stay in the Word of God. Outside the Word of God, Christians cannot be constantly nourished by God. A weakened state will leave men open to the attacks of the enemy.

Not all of us are in the ministry, but all of us are ministers if we are Christians. Because that is true, we must all remain close to the Word of God. Christ had good reason to say, "It is written: 'Man does not live on bread alone, but on every word that comes from the mouth of God' " (Matt. 4:4).

We must understand the importance of God's Word. In this life, only one thing is needful—God. If we are to live according to His Word, we must be in His Word.

Be intentional about developing a personal time each day. By committing to and following through with these steps, you will be able to remain in the Word.

Step 1: Plan a Place

Plan a specific place where you will be able to go to every day to meet the Lord. Maintaining a regular devotion is difficult if you constantly shift the location. Designate a spot in your house, at work, or the garage where you can spend time with God regularly.

Where do you intend to go? _____

Step 2: Plan a Time

Once you have established the place, designate the time. With a constantly filled schedule, you need to make your devotion time a regular priority. Do not try to slip it in whenever you have a free minute. You will never have a free minute. The time must be free of distractions and responsibilities. You must be able to sit quietly for a few moments without worrying about the phone, the kids, or the work in front of you. This is a time for God alone.

When do you intend to have your devotions? _____

Step 3: Make a Prayer List

Have a plan for what you are going to pray about to enable you to concentrate on the task at hand. If you do not specifically pray for something, your mind will probably wander from the office to the front lawn to the ball game and back. It is important that you record specific requests.

Use the following guide as a model:

Prayer Request	Date	Answer to Prayer	Date
_____ - _____		_____ - _____	

It is important to pray specifically. Rather than saying, "Lord, bless my family," pray, "Lord, help my wife in the struggle she is experiencing with…." If you do this, you will be able to see God answer your prayer specifically.

These simple methods of making God's Word an important part of your life will bear much fruit. As you strive to finish strong, you need to remain in God's Word every day. Those who think they don't need or don't have time for daily time with God in His Word come to regret that decision.

Write a brief prayer, asking God to help you be faithful in reading His Word.

_____

_____

_____

DAY 3
Be Accountable

Read Hebrews 4:12-13.

We discussed yesterday Hendricks' study of 246 ministers who had fallen into sexual immorality. The first characteristic these men shared was a lack of personal time spent in God's Word. Today we will discuss the second reason for their failure: lack of personal accountability. Each of these ministers had no personal accountability with another person. They had no one to encourage them on the path of righteousness.

How do you define *accountability*? Accountability is _____

_____

One of the best definitions of *accountability* is "a willingness to explain your actions." When a person explains to someone else what they are engaging in, that person is demonstrating a willingness to be accountable. It is vital to us as Christians to be accountable to someone as well as to hold ourselves accountable to Christ. For Christians, it is vital to our salvation that we are accountable to someone.

On a scale of 1 to 10 (1 being the lowest), how well do you like the idea of someone being accountable to you?

_____

On a scale of 1 to 10 (1 being the lowest), how well do you like being held accountable? _____

For Christian men the idea of accountability is appealing. However, when it comes to being held accountable, most men find it unbearable. It is difficult to be held to someone else's standard. Often we aren't nearly as hard on ourselves as someone else might be. We would rather be accountable only to ourselves.

Christian men must practice accountability with each other. Hebrews 4:12-13 tells us why accountability between Christians is so important. God will hold us accountable for our actions. If we learn to help each other stay true to the standard, we will begin to learn how to stand before God with integrity.

God knows your every thought and every feeling. Nothing can be hidden from Him. If you can develop a willingness to explain your actions before other men, your willingness to be honest before God will greatly increase. Denial is a great tool of the enemy. God wants you to be honest with yourself. When you stop deceiving yourself, you begin to live a life of honesty.

Hebrews 4 describes God's ability to see all things. The Word of God is described as being sharper than any double-edged sword; it penetrates even to dividing soul and spirit, joints and marrow; and judges the thoughts and attitudes of the heart. Because we must all give an account for ourselves and our desires, it is crucial that we develop a willing spirit now.

Where does accountability begin? Accountability begins in the home. It is developed by constant attention to honesty and openness in our relationships at home. If you practice deceit to those who are closest to you, your life is a lie. If you make excuses for the sins you commit or justify them with rationality, you are living a lie. Accountability begins with honesty.

Ask yourself the following questions:

How often do I say one thing and do another? (circle one)   Rarely   Sometimes   Often

Do any sins exist in my life that I have continually justified? (circle one)   Yes   No

If so, would explaining my actions to someone else help me recognize and deal with these sins? (circle one) Yes No

In order to be accountable, you must be willing to share your live with another person. Confession to God is wonderful, but God can also use others to help hold you to a standard. This type of accountability encourages humility, honesty, love, forgiveness, and hope.

No one can go it alone in the Christian life. The Lord has given us each other so that we can help each other on the journey. As soon as someone takes himself out of the fold, he is open to the attacks of the evil one. God would have us support and encourage each other. God would have us hold each other accountable.

List the names of one or more men with whom you would be willing to become an accountability partner:

_____

_____

If you are not willing, what would it take for you to become willing?

_____

Write a prayer, asking God to help you find that person or persons who will keep you accountable. Ask God to give you the strength to be humble and honest.

_____

_____

_____

DAY 4
Avoid Entanglements

Read Proverbs 5:21-23.

Hendricks stated that the third reason 246 ministers fell into sexual immorality was because they counseled women. Each of these men allowed himself to be in situations where emotional and physical entanglements were possible.

The frightening reality is if you are around women other than your wife in any situation, you are subject to temptation. As a Christian, you must be extremely careful in your relationships.

Christian men must keep their distance both emotionally and physically. Why is it so important to keep your distance? Your commitment to God and to your wife is at stake. If you are not cautious with your social relationships, you may end up jeopardizing your family relationships.

Men receive mixed messages from our culture about sexuality. You need to understand what you believe and will accept in order to interpret these messages. Answer the following questions:

Is it all right to be emotionally involved with a woman other than your wife? (circle)   Yes   No

How much does your religious belief guide your attitude toward sex? (circle) Not much   Some   A lot

Should sex be restricted to marriage? (circle) No   Depends   Yes

If not, when is sex appropriate? _____

How important is faithfulness within marriage? (circle) Not very important   Important   Very important

What is your attitude toward pornography? _____

One major reason many men do not finish strong is because of their attitudes toward sex. The world has made men compromise what the Scriptures say. The enemy has deceived thousands into believing what God intended no longer applies. Instead of influencing the world toward right beliefs, Christians are being corrupted by wrong beliefs.

A recent, carefully controlled study of nearly 3500 men and women provided some insight to the thinking of a number of conservative Christian men. The findings were shockingly eye-opening.

Researchers divided respondents into three categories of attitudes toward sex: traditional, relational, and recreational.
- The *traditional* group said that religious belief always guides their sexual behavior and that premarital, extramarital, and homosexual sex is wrong.
- The *relational* group believed that sex should be part of a loving relationship but should not necessarily be restricted to marriage.
- The *recreational* proponents believed sex should be enjoyed for its own sake and didn't necessarily have anything to do with love.

Here's the bombshell. Only 50.5 percent of conservative Protestants fall into the traditional category. *"That means that half of evangelical Christians believe sex does not necessarily have to be restricted to marriage"* (*Finishing Strong*, 63).

Look back at your answers. Which category do you fall into? _____

If your attitude about sex is casual, your ability to withstand sexual temptation will be weak. The Lord tells us to avoid evil, to flee immorality. If you do not understand what is immoral, you are bound to be swallowed up by evil.

That is where the problem lies. Scripture plainly teaches what is right and wrong about sexuality. It is no wonder so many men fall to sexual immorality and ruin their lives. They don't follow what the Word of God teaches.

The same study looked at the area of sexual faithfulness within marriage. Conservative Protestants came in second to last in faithfulness, just ahead of those with no religious affiliation. In regard to pornography, *41 percent* of all men reported having engaged in some type of pornography over the last 12 months (*Finishing Strong*, 64).

Christian men are in trouble. Unless we correct our attitudes toward sexuality, we are going to continue to fall to sexual temptation. We must guard ourselves emotionally as well as physically. Do not get emotionally involved with any woman other than your wife. To do so only invites trouble.

Label the following situations S for stay away, N for neutral, or B for become involved.
____ 1. One of your coworkers is having marital trouble and needs to talk.
____ 2. You have been asked to counsel a new Christian who is a woman about your age.
____ 3. You and a woman who is not your wife have been assigned as a visiting team one night a week.
____ 4. A neighbor lady has asked you to do some repairs around her house that will take several evenings. You agree because she is recently divorced.

Many men who fall to sexual immorality are not looking for trouble. They do not realize what is happening until it is too late. Don't let this happen to you. Use extreme caution in your relationships. Look to God for strength and guidance.

Pray: *"Father, help me to remain faithful to You and to my wife. Let Your Holy Spirit be my guide in my relationships. Help me to avoid evil and do what is good all the days of my life. Amen."*

DAY 5
Recognize Pridefulness

Read Proverbs 16:18-22.

The ministers studied by Hendricks all had one more characteristic in common about their sexual immorality; all 246 said, "I never thought it would happen to me." This reaction is typical of people caught in immorality; they didn't think it would happen. Most people cannot fathom ever making such a huge mistake in regard to their spirituality or the consequences to their families. This attitude is called *pride*.

This entire series will be of no value to a man who believes he is somehow exempt from the temptations and failings of most men. Only the man who understands his weaknesses and has the humility to accept correction can grow and become a stronger child of God. Pride weakens a person's ability to grow and change for the better.

The ministers in Hendrick's study never intended to sin against God. Sin in any form usually begins small. If it goes unchecked, it then grows into immoral behavior Christian men should abhor. The enemy wants you to slip blindly into sin. That is one of his greatest tactics for destruction.

Answer the following questions honestly:
Is it possible you could get involved emotionally with a woman other than your wife? (circle) Yes   No

Is it possible you could get involved physically with a woman other than your wife? (circle) Yes   No

Is it possible that you could leave your family for a relationship with another woman? (circle)   Yes   No

Any or all of these things might happen to you. If you think that it cannot happen, you are deceiving yourself. The statistics show that most men who cheat on their wives at some time in their relationship never intended to do it. The good news is that it doesn't have to happen. If you give your life over to God daily, ask Him for strength and guidance, and commit yourself to your wife, you can beat the odds and live a godly life in Christ. You simply have to be willing to do what God wants you to do. This takes all the strength you have, but it is the most rewarding task you will ever undertake.

What does God want men to do?
- Stay in the Scriptures.
- Stay close to a godly friend.
- Stay away from emotional or physical relationships with other women.
- Stay humble and alert.

A man diligently practicing these things will be able to turn away from the flesh and unite himself to God. God wants you to take captive every thought and every action. This is the goal of the Christian life.

Why do so many men fail to finish strong? They fall to the deception that the grass is always greener on the other side. They believe the devil's lies about what men really need and about what God wants to keep from them. They have pride in their own abilities and can fool themselves into thinking they have done nothing wrong.

The apostle Paul wrote "Do not think of yourself more highly than you ought" (Rom. 12:3). The higher we are in God's grace, the lower we seem to be in our own esteem. I am not seeking to promote not self-depreciation, but rather a realization of God's amazing grace. The more we realize the gift of God's presence in our lives, the more we love Him for saving us though we are sinners.

The more you understand the danger of pride, the more you will beg God to keep you from it. It is helpful to ask God every day to humble you. Label the following situations with H (an example of humility) or P (an example of pride.

____ 1. Ralph was asked to step down as chairman of an important church committee that he had headed for 13 years in order to rotate committee terms. Ralph was hurt and vowed to fight this move.

____ 2. James asked his son for forgiveness for having lost his temper. He shared this failure with a prayer partner.

____ 3. The pastor asked the men of the church to come forward and pray at the altar. Justin stayed at his place in the pew. "Nobody can tell me when I need to pray, how, or where," he fumed.

____ 4. Edward had never missed a day of work in six years. Even though he had a cold and temperature, he went to work.

____ 5. Rick knew he had hurt his wife's feelings. He rationalized why she didn't deserve an explanation or apology. "I'm not giving in to her tears. She can just get over it."

Pride is a doorway to all sin. If a man can learn to be humble before God, that man will be close to the heart of God. Jesus said, "Blessed are the poor in spirit" (Matt. 5:3).

As we finish this series, remember that God has given you everything you need to succeed as a man in this world. You lack nothing that you will not receive from Him. Follow the ways of God and allow Him to give you life eternal with our blessed Lord and Savior, Jesus Christ.

Pray the following prayer:

"Have mercy on me Lord in my weakness. You know the sins I struggle with daily. I ask that You would create in me a clean heart and renew my spirit within me. I thank You for everything You have given me, and I pray that I will be a faithful servant to You all the days of my life. Bless my family and enable me to love them as You love the world. In Your precious and holy name, Amen."

END NOTES

Chapter 2

[1]Willard F. Harley, Jr., *His Needs Her Needs* (Grand Rapids, MI: Fleming H. Revell, 1994) 12-13.
[2]Gary Rosberg, *Guard Your Heart* (Sisters, OR: Multnomah, 1994) 123-128.

Chapter 5

[1]Neil J. Salkind and Sueann Robinson Ambron, *Child Development* (New York: Holt, Rinehart and Winston, 1987) 415 (attributed to A.C. Huston).

Chapter 6

[1]Charles Colson and Nancy Pearson, *How Now Shall We Live?* (Nashville, TN: LifeWay Press, 1999).

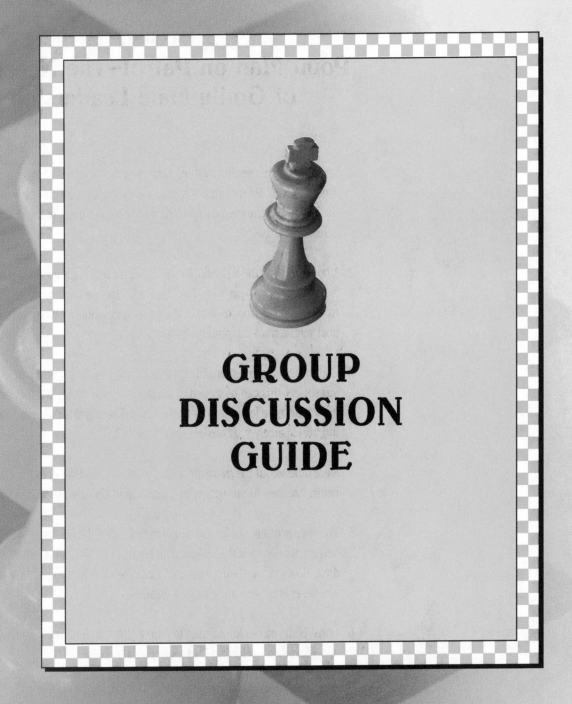

GROUP
DISCUSSION
GUIDE

Session 1
Point Man on Patrol—The Necessity of Godly Male Leadership

1. Steve begins this session by discussing the crisis of male leadership in America today. He specifically says that men no longer know how to lead in the home, the church, or in society. What do you think are the main causes behind this crisis?

2. A *point man* is the individual responsible for leading a group of soldiers. He is the one person who all those behind him look to for direction. How is the man of a family supposed to take on this responsibility? What are some practical ways a man can lead his family?

3. God has given the responsibility for leadership in the home to the man. In our society, this can be viewed as sexist and chauvinistic. What is the biblical model for male leadership in the home and how is this different from what the world perceives? (Consider Eph. 5:25-33.)

4. Steve talks about the *neutralization* of men today. How does the enemy neutralize men in our society and what ramifications are created by this?

5. The enemy has a two-fold strategy for destroying the family—to alienate and eventually sever the relationship between a man and his wife and children. How are men being alienated from their families today? How successful has the enemy been at destroying families?

6. Christ is the model for all men to follow. How can a man take the leadership of his family by following Christ's example?

Assignment: Take some time this week to evaluate your family. What type of leader in the home are you? Think of specific ways you can overcome the enemy's attempt to alienate you from your family.

Session 2
The Tasks of Husbands

1. We live in an age where the commitment to marriage is not taken very seriously. Why do you think divorce is so acceptable in our society today? What do you think the future of marriage will be?

2. The husband has many roles to fulfill. As a group try to list a few of the roles of husbands. In order to fulfill these roles, a husband must possess certain characteristics. List a few characteristics of a good husband and tell why they are necessary.

3. Men and women are different to say the least. As a man, how difficult is it to understand women and why do you feel this is true? What are some of the most difficult differences to deal with?

4. Women today are more independent and self-sufficient than ever before. What kind of needs do women have today? How does a husband meet those needs?

5. What does the biblical model of marriage look like? How can we make our own marriages resemble that model?

Assignment: As a husband, you are responsible for understanding and honoring your wife. As you complete the individual studies this week, share with your wife specific reactions to what you are learning. Think of ways you can meet her needs more appropriately.

Session 3
Anchoring Your Family Chain

1. In this session, Steve talks about *drifting families*. He describes them as being families who lack a solid foundation to stand on. With what do you think most people are trying to anchor their families? Are these types of anchors working? Why or why not?

2. For a man to truly anchor his family, he must be anchored in Christ. Once he is secure, he will be able to steady his family against the world. How do you try not only to anchor yourself, but also to anchor your family in Christ? Is this working?

3. God has given the responsibility of leadership to men. This makes many men very uncomfortable and they try to escape the responsibility. Why is it that God has given this duty to men and not to women? How are our homes and churches being affected by men who fail to lead?

4. Most men today work very hard at providing for their families' financial and physical needs. What are you doing to provide for your family's spiritual needs? Steve points out our calling to anchor our families for the next 100 years. What are you doing today to give your children the Christian heritage you possess?

Assignment: Take time this week to talk with your wife and children about where your family is headed. It is important that you have a vision for your family's future. Begin by discussing your family's background and beliefs. Encourage your wife and children to talk about where they see the family headed.

Session 4
The Seven Steps of Fathering

1. In session 4, Steve speaks about the way fathering has changed over the last few decades. How is the way you father different from the methods of your own father or grandfather? Do you think children are being affected in a positive or negative way because of this change? Why?

2. One of the first rules of fathering is that a father must be active in his responsibility. A father must take the initiative when it comes to raising his children. How do you think passivity by fathers today has affected children? How does this passivity change the roles of the parents in these families?

3. Discipline today is a very volatile subject. With so many parents being accused of abusing their children, it is often dangerous for a man to discipline his children. What are the main differences between abuse and discipline? How can a father discipline his children correctly?

4. Truly great fathers can never be accused of neglect. Today many fathers work so hard to provide for their families, their families rarely get to spend much time together. Briefly discuss the affects of negligence on children and ways of preventing this from happening within your families.

5. Steve speaks about *teachable moments*. Recall some moments you have gone through with your children in which you were able to be a teacher.

Assignment: Evaluate your fathering abilities. Seriously consider how much time you spend with your children and what sacrifices you are making for them. Share any insights with your wife and children this week.

Session 5
Raising Masculine Sons and Feminine Daughters

1. In this session, Steve addresses the issues of masculinity and femininity. It is an issue that is becoming increasingly confusing as men and women change identities and roles. What do you think masculinity entails? Do most men meet the standard of masculinity today? Why or why not?

2. Children look primarily to the father as they develop their personal identities and gender roles. What type of characteristics do you want to instill in your sons? What type of characteristics do you want to give your daughters? How will these characteristics affect their relationship with society?

3. Steve quotes the sociologist Steve Clark in this session. Clark discusses the feminization of Christianity and the types of characteristics we most readily identify with being Christian. Do you think Christian men have been feminized and if so, what does God want Christian men to act like?

4. The father is key in the development of the daughter. What types of virtues are you giving your daughters? What kind of example are you for your daughters as they begin to relate to the opposite sex?

5. In week 5, Steve states that the roles of men and women are predetermined. He believes that the man should be the primary provider in the family and the woman the primary caregiver. Do you agree with this concept and do you think it is possible to implement in the world today?

Assignment: As you work on the lessons this week, define your perception of the roles of men and women. Discuss with your wife the biblical idea of the family and think of ways of bringing your family into this shape.

Session 6
Understanding the Times

1. In session 6, Steve talks about some of the fundamental problems within our society. The first issue he addresses is the stripping away of our nation's foundations. What do you think will be the consequences our country will face if it continues to reject the God, the Bible, and the absolute truth on which it was founded?

2. What kind of country do you think your children will live in? Do you believe that Christianity will still be the prominent religion in America when your grandchildren are living here? What are you doing to provide a solid foundation for your children to stand on as they enter these dark times?

3. Steve discusses the idea of *moral relativism*. Are you or your family being affected by this philosophy? In what way? How is the morality of your children different from your own?

4. How do you feel God is going to judge the United States for its actions and philosophies? Many people are waiting for a revival to sweep the nation. Do you believe this might happen and if so, what will the state of Christianity be like after it has occurred?

Assignment: Because of the moral degeneration our country is going through, it is more important than ever that you give your family the strong moral structure they will need to succeed in life. This week, ask your family some very important questions:
- What do they believe about God?
- Do they feel truth is essential to life?
- What is their attitude toward sexuality today?
- What things are they going to pursue in life and why?

If you are able to be open and honest with your children, they can be honest with you. Discuss why it is important to have a Christian mindset and what hope there is in Jesus.

Session 7
A One-Woman Kind of Man

1. Many Christians fail to realize the difficulty and seriousness of being a Christian. They coast through life having a faith that functions but that does little to really change the way they live. In 1 Timothy 1:18, we read that we are to fight the good fight. What are we exactly fighting against and what do we hope to win?

2. Steve speaks seriously about the way God uses a man's conscience to keep him from sin. In what ways do people try to dull their conscience? What effect does this loss of moral feeling have on our society?

3. In session 7, Steve addresses the issue of faithfulness. Christian men are to be faithful to their wives with their minds, eyes, and entire bodies. If a man practices this type of faithfulness, how will he grow in his likeness to God? Specifically, what is being changed in a man? Why does the world see lust as being acceptable?

4. How do men objectify women? Why does God want us to treat women as fellow heirs of grace? How will this attitude change the way we see and treat women?

Assignment: As you go through this week, notice the way you think about women. Do you let your mind fantasize about other women? Write specific attitudes you have that you need to let God change. Write ways of dealing with temptation before you encounter it. In your prayers, pray specifically that God will enable you to overcome lust and be a one-woman kind of man.

Session 8
Finishing Strong

1. Many people have a difficult time seeing long-term. In our country, instant gratification is becoming an expected convenience. In the Christian life, much of what we desire takes time to develop. Hebrews 12:1 likens the Christian life to a race that must be run with endurance. In your experience, how difficult is it to endure in the race and what ways have you found that are helpful in renewing your strength?

2. Many people fail to finish strong in the Christian life. What reasons do you think would cause a person to leave the faith or lose the enthusiasm they began with?

3. Steve suggests four ways to defeat failure in the Christian life. A man must stay in the Scriptures, stay accountable, stay away from emotional ties to other women, and stay humble. Discuss how each of these suggestions can help a man stay on track.

Assignment: Write a personal mission statement this week. Make time to get together and share with others your personal statement. This will allow you to share personally with others as well as acquire some accountability partners.

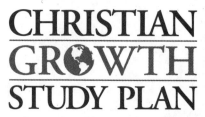

CHRISTIAN GROWTH STUDY PLAN

Preparing Christians to Serve

In the **Christian Growth Study Plan (formerly Church Study Course),** this book *Men Leading the Charge: God's Game Plan for the Family* is a resource for course credit in the subject area Personal Life of the Christian Growth category of diploma plans. To receive credit, read the book, complete the learning activities, show your work to your pastor, a staff member, or church leader, then complete the following information. This page may be duplicated. Send the completed page to:

Christian Growth Study Plan
127 Ninth Avenue, North, MSN 117
Nashville, TN 37234-0117
FAX: (615)251-5067

For information about the Christian Growth Study Plan, refer to the current Christian Growth Study Plan Catalog. Your church office may have a copy. If not, request a free copy from the Christian Growth Study Plan office (615/251-2525).

Men Leading the Charge: God's Game Plan for the Family
COURSE NUMBER: CG-0605

PARTICIPANT INFORMATION

Social Security Number (USA ONLY)	Personal CGSP Number*	Date of Birth (MONTH, DAY, YEAR)

Name (First, Middle, Last)	Home Phone

Address (Street, Route, or P.O. Box)	City, State, or Province	Zip/Postal Code

CHURCH INFORMATION

Church Name

Address (Street, Route, or P.O. Box)	City, State, or Province	Zip/Postal Code

CHANGE REQUEST ONLY

☐ Former Name

☐ Former Address	City, State, or Province	Zip/Postal Code

☐ Former Church	City, State, or Province	Zip/Postal Code

Signature of Pastor, Conference Leader, or Other Church Leader	Date

*New participants are requested but not required to give SS# and date of birth. Existing participants, please give CGSP# when using SS# for the first time. Thereafter, only one ID# is required. **Mail to:** Christian Growth Study Plan, 127 Ninth Ave., North, Nashville, TN 37234-0117. Fax: (615)251-5067

Rev. 6-99